I0179731

AUSSI/OR

ISBN (print): 978-1-916541-18-4
ISBN (ebook): 978-1-916541-19-1

First edition.

First published in 2025 by Erratum Press
Sheffield, UK
www.erratumpress.com

Design and typesetting by Ansgar Allen

AUSSI/OR

Un Coup de dés Down Under

Toby Fitch

ERRATUM PRESS
ACADEMIC DIVISION

Other works by Toby Fitch

Poetry Books

Object Permanence: Calligrammes (Puncher & Wattmann, 2022)
Sydney Spleen (Giramondo Publishing, 2021)
Where Only the Sky had Hung Before (Vagabond Press, 2019)
Object Permanence: Selected Calligrammes (Penteract Press, 2019)
ILL LIT POP (Cerberus Press/Flying Islands Books, 2018)
The Bloomin' Notions of Other & Beau (Vagabond Press, 2016)
Jerilderies (Vagabond Press, 2014)
Rawshock (Puncher & Wattmann, 2012)

Chapbooks

Born to Creep (Stale Objects dePress, 2018)
Undulating Cloud Sonnet (Stale Objects dePress, 2017)
Quarrels (Stale Objects dePress, 2013)
Everyday Static (Rare Objects #52, Vagabond Press, 2010)

Anthologies (as Editor)

Groundswell: The Overland *Judith Wright Poetry Prize for New and Emerging Poets 2007–2020*
Best of Australian Poems 2021 (co-edited with Ellen van Neerven)

Acknowledgements

An earlier, shorter version of this essay was written with the financial assistance of an Australian Postgraduate Award and made up part of a Doctor of Arts (Creative PhD) thesis at the University of Sydney titled, 'Themparks: Alternative Play in Contemporary Australian Poetry', awarded in 2017. That shorter version of the essay was then published by *Cordite Poetry Review* in 2018. I would like to thank the retired Dr Bruce Gardiner and Associate Professor David Brooks for their supervision, as well as Justin Clemens, Susan M. Schultz, Louis Armand, Peter Minter and Matthew Hall for their feedback or editorial advice.

List of Illustrations

1. INTRODUCTION 3

2. EXPOSITION 18

3. CHRISTOPHER BRENNAN: "MUSICOPOEMATOGRAPHOSCOPE" 27

4. CHRIS EDWARDS: "A FLUKE" 38

5. JOHN TRANTER: "DESMOND'S COUPÉ" 55

6. DEVELOPMENT 62

7. RECAPITULATION 89

8. CODA 103

Bibliography

List of Illustrations

Front cover illustration: Brownian Motion, in Jean Perrin, *Atoms* (1916).

Figure 1. A representation of Brownian Motion, in Jean Perrin, *Atoms* (1916).

Figure 2. "Schema" by Dan Graham, in Doherty (ed.), *Aspen Magazine in a Box [for Stéphane Mallarmé]* (1967).

Figure 3. Cover of Marcel Broodthaers' redacted edition of *Un Coup de dés jamais n'abolira le hasard* (1969).

Figure 4. Double-page spread from Broodthaers' *Un Coup de dés* (lithograph on transparent paper).

Figure 5. The title page of Christopher Brennan's *Prose-Verse-Poster-Algebraic-Symbolico-Riddle Musicopoematographoscope* (1981).

Figure 6. A double-page spread from "Musicopoematographoscope".

Figure 7. The final line of "Musicopoematographoscope".

Figure 8. Nicholas Desprez, Lorenz Attractor, *Chaoscope* (2009), http://www.chaoscope.org/gallery.htm.

Figure 9. Paul Bourke, Lorenz Attractor, *The Lorenz Attractor in 3D* (1997), http://paulbourke.net/fractals/lorenz/.

Figure 10. Final double-page spread of *Un Coup de dés.*

Figure 11. Final double-page spread of "A Fluke".

Figure 12. Casper the Friendly Ghost (with cat), screenshot from *Casper the Friendly Ghost* (New York: Famous Studios, 1945).

Figure 13. Unicron eats the Death Star, *Deviant Art*, 2012: http://profkilljoy7z.deviantart.com/art/Unicron-Eats-the-Deathstar-325554426.

Figure 14. A still from Loïe Fuller's *La danse des couleurs*, as conceived by Brygida Ochaim (1988).

Figure 15. Cheshire Cat, screenshot from *Alice in Wonderland* (Burbank: Walt Disney Studios, 1951).

Figure 16. Konrad Polthier, Klein Bottle, "Imaging Maths—Inside the Klein Bottle", *Plus Magazine* (2003): https://plus.maths.org/content/os/issue26/features/mathart/kleinBottle_anim.

Figure 17. Timescape of Arthur Rubinstein's 1939 recording of Chopin's *Mazurka Op. 68 No. 3*, *CHARM: AHRC* (2009): http://www.charm.rhul.ac.uk/projects/p2_3_2.html.

Figure 18. Dušan I. Bjelić, Freud's Chemistry of Words, in "Balkan Geography and the De-Orientalization of Freud" (2011): 37.

Figure 19. Theodoros Pelecanos, drawing of an ouroboros in a 1478 copy of a lost alchemical tract by Synesius, in *Codex Parisinus graecus 2327* in the Bibliothèque Nationale, France.

Figure 20. Caravaggio, *Head of Medusa*, oil on canvas mounted on wood, 60 x 50 cm, Florence: Uffizi Gallery (1597).

Figure 21. The first (single) page of Chris Edwards' *After Naptime* (2014), 7.

Figure 22. A double-page spread from *After Naptime*, 10–11.

Figure 23. A double-page spread from *After Naptime*, 18–19.

Figure 24. Athanasius Kircher, Map of the "lost" island of Atlantis, in *Mundus subterraneus*, Amsterdam (1665), 82, Rare Maps: https://www.raremaps.com/gallery/detail/20754.

Where a full citation does not appear above, see related footnotes or the bibliography.

If reading the print edition in black and white, see the open access edition in full colour, downloadable at Erratum Press (Academic Division).

1

aussi

The French adverb *aussi* means "also", "in addition", "as well", and "too". It is also used as a comparative, as in "as", as an exclamatory "so", and also at the beginning of sentences as a "therefore", or "consequently". Its English homophone is "Aussie", of course. And its meaning of "too", T double-O, might fancifully be taken for the English number "two", its double, or even the French *tu* = you.

or

The French noun *or* is two different words with two different Latin origins: one, from Latin *aurum* (and popularly *orum*), is a noun meaning "gold" (with adjective, "golden"); the other, from Latin *hora*, is a conjunction meaning "now", "but", "in fact", "as it happens" and, more rarely, "thus" or "therefore"; its doublet is *heure* = "hour".[1] In English heraldry, "or" also means gold. The English homonym for *or* is obviously "or", that infinitely useful word that links alternatives, but we also have "ore", "awe", "oar", and "aw". From Middle English, "or" is a reduced form of the obsolete conjunction *other* (which superceded Old English *oththe*). "Or" can also be found as a suffix in English nouns denoting a person or thing with agency: "escalator", "resistor", or "conductor".[2]

or

While setting up for much play on the homonymic, homophonic and homographic, these terms are not quite synonymous, and yet all are used as poetic techniques by the protagonists to come in this essay. Part of the interest in the Australian versions of Mallarmé (as with the language-play of Joyce and Freud and Lacan too!—all *also* yet to come) is that the

[1] Auguste Brachet, *An Etymological Dictionary of the French Language*, trans. G. W. Kitchin (Oxford: Clarendon, 1873).

[2] *Oxford English Dictionary*, 2nd ed., 20 vols (Oxford: Oxford University Press, 1989).

aural and visual, or the phonic and graphic, are at once bound together yet come apart, which this work hopes to make something of (*poeisis*) along the way and with regard to the context of settler Australian poetry and its self-negation, or tendency to anti-poetry, later in the piece. For now, the homophonic is the predominant mode of soundplay, and so the "homophone" will be the term that dialectically (or not) sublates the others, however gnomic that might sound or appear.

aussi

Un Coup de dés by Stephane Mallarmé, that gnomic poem of the late nineteenth century (1897), full of esoteric symbolism and disjointed syntax, that exploded from the left margin across the gutters of eleven double-page spreads in scattered fragments—like *disjecta membra*—visual, musical, collage-like, and typographically diverse, looks like many things on the page: rocks emerging from the white foam of the sea; ash on the table to be swished about by some diviner; a mobile, hung across a child's crib; threads or strings blown in the wind; constellations in the night sky.

aussi

There are two representations of the "Big Dipper" (U.S.) or "The Plough" (U.K.) in the poem's fragments. The Big Dipper is an asterism that represents the seven brightest stars of the northern hemisphere constellation *Ursa Major*.

or

The poem's words on the page could even be seen as a representation of Brownian Motion (or pedesis, from Greek: πήδησις /pɛ̌ːdɛːsis/ "leaping"), which is the random motion of particles suspended in a fluid resulting from their collision with the quick atoms or molecules in the gas or liquid. The term "Brownian motion" can also refer to the mathematical model used to describe such random movements, which is often called a particle theory.[3]

[3] Albert Einstein, *Investigations on the Theory of the Brownian Movement*, trans. A. D. Cowper, 1926 (Mineola: Dover, 1956), http://users.physik.fu-berlin.de/~kleinert/files/eins_brownian.pdf.

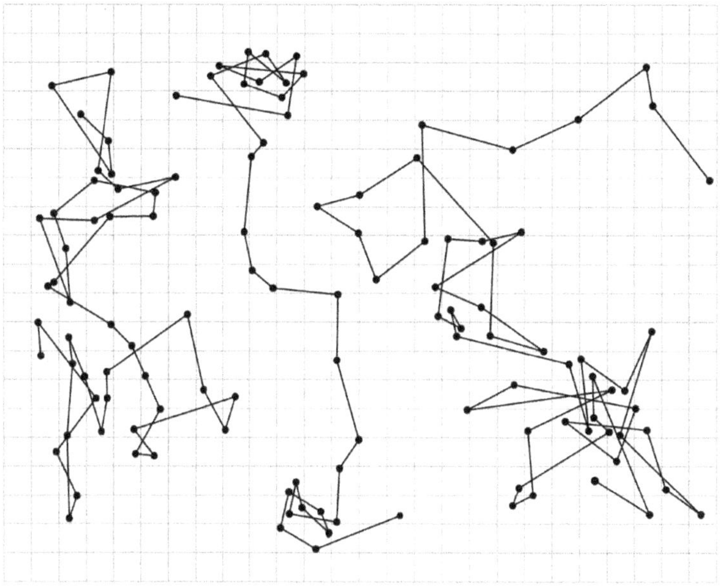

Fig. 1. A representation of Brownian Motion.[4]

or

The atomic law of the clinamen—the minimal swerve of an atom in laminar flow. Jed Rasula and Steve McCaffery, evoking Lucretius' use of the clinamen in literature, compare the movement of atoms to the movement of letters: "Atoms ... are to bodies what letters are to words: heterogeneous, deviant, and combinatory". Citing Paul Valéry, who saw the words in *Un Coup de dés* as "atoms of time that serve as the germs of infinite consequences lasting through psychological centuries", Rasula and McCaffery then note:

> The spaciousness evoked here is a reminder that, in Epicurean cosmology, the contextual prerequisite of atoms is a void. We might say by analogy that void is to atoms what space and *différence* are to

4 Reproduced from the book *Les Atomes* (1914) by Jean Baptiste Perrin, three tracings of the motion of colloidal particles of radius 0.53 μm, as seen under a microscope. Successive positions every 30 seconds are joined by straight line segments (the mesh size is 3.2 μm). Jean Perrin, *Atoms* (London: Constable, 1916), 115.

> letters. Mallarmé's spacing in *Un Coup de dés* solicits—as integral to the experience and the eventual dice-throw of the poem—the backing of that void (the ground of emergent figures) through which the lettristic swerves disseminate.[5]

aussi

Its full title, *UN COUP DE DÉS JAMAIS N'ABOLIRA LE HASARD* ("A THROW OF THE DICE WILL [N]EVER ABOLISH CHANCE")[6]—perhaps a serious interpretation of probability—describes the event of the poem and, like dice, its words bounce or leap through the double-page spreads[7] in corresponding large and capitalised typeface: *UN COUP DE DÉS* ("A THROW OF THE DICE") appears alone as a title page, *JAMAIS* ("WILL [N]EVER") appears on the following spread with a few fragments of text below it, *N'ABOLIRA* (ABOLISH) three spreads later with much more surrounding text, while *LE HASARD* ("CHANCE") rounds out the phrase a further four spreads on, marooned in the most chaotic double spread of the book (in terms of the number and variety of particles on the page), two spreads from the end. Every fragment of the poem that falls around this title, thrown across the sea of pages in variously sized typeface, switching between roman, italic and capital letters, unravels and overlays in what Alain Badiou describes as "a stupefying series of metaphorical translations around the theme of the undecidable".[8] Or, as Mallarmé dubs it in his Preface: "prismatic subdivisions of the Idea"—lines of text, if read from the upper left, across the book's gutter, to the lower right, "speed up and slow down the movement ... intimating it

5 Jed Rasula and Steve McCaffery, eds., *Imagining Language: An Anthology* (Cambridge: MIT Press, 1998), 532–3.

6 I have translated *JAMAIS* as "[N]EVER" to preserve both possible meanings of *jamais*, "never" and "ever".

7 "Page openings" is the common bibliographical term, but for the purposes of this essay I will use Chris Edwards' "double-page spreads", or "double spreads". He employs the term "double-page spread" to describe Mallarmé's "unit of composition" in *Un Coup de dés*. See Chris Edwards, "Double Talk" (paper presented at the Sydney Poetry Seminar on "Poetry and Authenticity", May 20–21, 2005), *Poetry International Web* (Nov 1, 2006), http://www.poetryinternationalweb.net/pi/site/cou_article/item/7929/Double-Talk/en.

8 Alain Badiou, *Being and Event*, 1998, trans. Oliver Feltham (New York: Continuum, 2005), 194.

through a simultaneous vision of the Page."[9] Within these subdivisions, fragmented images surface as remnants of some lost-at-sea narrative, wavering, oscillating, vibrating throughout: the Master of a vessel, standing at the bottom of a shipwreck, his fist holding the dice shaking eternally at the stars, the lurching ship, a feather hovering over the Abyss, the proposed rolling of the dice between possible outcomes. "All Thought emits a Throw of the Dice", to quote the last line, yet, "A throw of the dice will never abolish chance"—a decisive act with a result determined by ever greater and obscure forces.[10]

or

Inertia.[11]

or

Henry Weinfield, one of Mallarmé's translators, sums up the various angles from which to read *Un Coup de dés*: "What is allegorised ... is the ebb and flow of humanity's continual struggle to seize hold of the Absolute: the Master-Seaman's confrontation with the oceanic abyss, the Poet's confrontation with the white page, the Philosopher's with the Void, and Everyman's with the 'wrecks and errors' (to borrow Ezra Pound's phrase) of experience."[12]

[9] Stéphane Mallarmé, *Collected Poems*, trans. and with a commentary by Henry Weinfield (Berkeley: University of California Press, 1996), 121.

[10] Mallarmé, "*Un Coup de dés*", *Collected Poems*, 144–5

[11] Inertia, in classical physics, can apply to a body in uniform motion or at rest. It was Isaac Newton's first law of motion from *Philosophiæ Naturalis Principia Mathematica*: "The *vis insita*, or innate force of matter, is a power of resisting by which every body, as much as in it lies, endeavours to preserve its present state, whether it be of rest or of moving uniformly forward in a straight line." Isaac Newton, *Newton's Principia: the mathematical principles of natural philosophy*, trans. Andrew Motte (New York: Daniel Adee, 1846), 72.

[12] Henry Weinfield, "Commentary", in Mallarmé, *Collected Poems*, 266–7. The Pound phrase is actually back to front. It comes from "Canto CXVI": "Tho' my errors and wrecks lie about me". See Ezra Pound, *The Cantos of Ezra Pound*, 1934 (New York: New Directions, 1993), 816.

aussi

When Paul Valéry first witnessed the event of *Un Coup de dés*, he remarked: "It seemed to me that I was looking at the form and pattern of a thought, placed for the first time in finite space. Here space itself truly spoke, dreamed, and gave birth to temporal forms",[13] which seems like a reaction that Theodor Adorno might have classified as "astonishment vis-à-vis what is beheld rather than vis-à-vis what it is about."[14] According to Immanuel Kant, however, space and time are nothing but forms of intuition; they are the base of all experience, à *priori*. We make non-empirical, singular, immediate representations of space and of time and it's only through these representations that we can experience things as distinct from ourselves/our inner mental states.[15] By this he means that we don't come to our understanding of space and time by first observing the objects we experience and then "by abstraction". Our sensibilities are a jumble of representations, and so our interpretations of a poem, which itself is contingent on language and how it's arranged on the page, is thus, always and already, a representation of a representation, a construction of a construction.

aussi

As Mallarmé wrote to André Gide, shortly after the poem was first published, likening the shape of the poem to a constellation locking into place: "the constellation will, fatally, assume, according to the precise laws and in so far as it's possible in a printed text, the form of a constellation. The ship will list from the top of one page to the bottom of the next, etc.: for, and this is the whole point … the rhythm of a sentence about an act or even an object has meaning only if it imitates them".[16]

[13] Weinfield, "Commentary", 265.

[14] Theodor Adorno, "Subject-Object", in *Aesthetic Theory*, 1970, trans. Robert Hullot-Kentor (Minneapolis: University of Minnesota Press, 1998), 225.

[15] Immanuel Kant, *Critique of Pure Reason*, 1781, trans. J. M. D. Meiklejohn (New York: Dover, 2003), 23–33.

[16] Mallarmé, "Letter to André Gide", May 14, 1897, in *Selected Letters of Stéphane Mallarmé*, ed. and trans. Rosemary Lloyd (Chicago: Chicago University Press, 1988), 223.

aussi

Negative space does the semantic inverse, according to Jacques Derrida, who suggests that the "rhythm" of the white spaces in *Un Coup de dés*—"as if without support"—succeeds in collapsing space and time:

> The white of the spacing has no determinate meaning, it does not simply belong to the plurivalence of all the other whites. More than or less than the polysemic series, a loss or excess of meaning, it folds up the text toward itself, and at each moment points out the place (where "nothing / will have taken place / except the place".[17]), the condition, the labor, the rhythm. As the page *folds in* upon itself, one will never be able to decide if *white* signifies something, or signifies only, or in addition, the space of writing itself.[18]

or

As Octavio Paz writes of Mallarmé: "The meaning does not reside outside the poem but within it, not in what the words say, but in what *they say to each other*".[19]

To which Mallarmé perhaps responds with his own (subjective) objective best: "This aim, I call Transposition; Structure, another … The pure work implies the disappearance of the poet speaking, who cedes the initiative to words, through the clash of their inequalities; they light each other up through reciprocal reflections".[20]

aussi

Mallarmé's modernist, or one might say pre-postmodernist, *Un Coup de dés* has been transposed into new forms and conceptions almost ad nauseum since its inception just prior to the twentieth century. Countless artists in

17 Mallarmé, *Collected Poems*, 142.

18 Jacques Derrida, "Mallarmé", 1974, trans. Christine Roulston, in *Acts of Literature*, ed. Derek Attridge (London: Routledge, 1991), 115–6.

19 Octavio Paz, *Alternating Current*, 1967, trans. Helen R. Lane (New York: Viking, 1967), 4.

20 Mallarmé, "Crisis of Verse", in *Divagations*, 1897, trans. Barbara Johnson (Cambridge: Belknap, 2007), 208.

particular—visual, sculptural, installation, performance, and conceptual artists—but also many musicians, film makers, and choreographers, have re-envisaged the poem, proving it to be, or propagating it to become, the hall of mirrors Mallarmé originally designed.

aussi

In 1912, Pablo Picasso alluded to *Un Coup de dés* in his collage, *Bouteille, verre et journal sur une table*, by truncating a newspaper headline from "UN COUP DE THÉÂTRE" to "UN COUP DE THÉ", highlighting the collage-like performativity of the poem. In 1929, Man Ray opened his short film *Les Mystères du Chateau de Dés* with a quotation from the poem and featured dice in the film's visual symbolism. In 1952, a series of black, white, grey and red paper collages by Hella Guth, *Un Coup de dés jamais n'abolira hasard: poème/par Stéphane Mallarmé*, foreshadowed future extensions into more three-dimensional and material techniques by dozens of conceptual, sculptural and cinematic artists. In 1967, Brian Doherty edited *Aspen Magazine in a Box [for Stéphane Mallarmé]*, a box of interchangeable mixed media works that featured essays by Roland Barthes ("The Death of the Author") and Susan Sontag ("The Aesthetics of Silence"), phonograph recordings (of John Cage, Merce Cunningham and Marcel Duchamp), and "maze models", among other mixed media, suggesting a constellated reading-viewing-listening-making experience of reciprocal reflections on Mallarméan notions. The box included Dan Graham's "Poem, March 1966", or *Schema*, a conceptual poem written specifically for art magazine publication to invert the gallery-to-magazine timeline of an artwork's representation (the poem is a literal schema for a textual artwork that would begin in the pages of a magazine, and then be transposed on to a gallery wall). It could otherwise be read as a schema for a poem of *Un Coup de dés*' spatial and temporal ilk:

SCHEMA

(number of) adjectives
(number of) adverbs
(percentage of) area not occupied by type
(percentage of) area occupied by type
(number of) columns
(number of) conjunctions
(number of) depression of type into surface of page
(number of) gerunds
(number of) infinitives
(number of) letters of alphabet
(number of) lines
(number of) mathematical symbols
(number of) nouns
(number of) numbers
(number of) participles
(perimeter of) page
(weight of) paper sheet
(type) paper stock
(thinness of of) paper stock
(number of) prepositions
(number of) pronouns
(number of point) size type
(name of) typeface
(number of) words
(number of) words capitalized
(number of) words italicized
(number of) words not capitalized
(number of) words not italicized

Fig. 2. "Schema" by Dan Graham.[21]

[21] Brian Doherty (ed.), *Aspen Magazine in a Box [for Stéphane Mallarmé][a.k.a. The Minimalism Issue]*, 5 + 6, Fall/Winter (1967).

aussi

Schema was followed in 1974 by Graham's Mallarméan homage *Present Continuous Past*, a video installation of mirrors, exhibited in the Centre Pompidou to the present day, in which the viewer becomes a participant in a continuous viewing of the recent past in the present moment (due to an eight-second delay). As with Mallarmé's *Le Livre* (which was also proposed to be a performance, not simply a conceptual Book) and the visual and syntactical reflexivity of *Un Coup de dés*, the work's coinciding of form, content and context, and its subversion of representation in time, challenges the viewer's notions of coherence and requires them to re-coordinate the relations between recorded and immediate experience, rendering any present moment undecidable.

Fig. 3: Cover of Marcel Broodthaers' redacted edition of *Un Coup de dés*.

aussi

In 1969, in perhaps the most notorious homage to *Un Coup de dés*, Marcel Broodthaers reproduced the Gallimard print edition but with its entire text redacted, censored, "to give us some underlying geometric shape or ontic insight"[22]—the only text in the edition (besides the text on the cover, which replaces "POÈME" with the word "IMAGE") appears in the Preface, where Broodthaers substitutes Mallarmé's introduction from *Cosmopolis* with the full text of *Un Coup de dés* in a block and with the poem's lines separated by forward slashes. At the exhibition *Exposition littéraire autour de Mallarmé: Marcel Broodthaers à la Deblioudebliou/S*, this reproduction was presented in three different forms for the gallery space—on anodised aluminum, on transparent mechanographic paper (the original edition), and on opaque paper—while in the background a tape recording of Broodthaers reading the poem played on a loop.

aussi

This multimedia homage would provoke dozens of artists to create redacted works of double-, triple- even quadruple-homage over the next few decades, among countless other types of extrapolation and transposition into other visual and performative artforms. The permutations seem endless, but there have been few that genuinely tamper with the French text, or manipulate the text to generate new text, besides of course the many translations, especially into English, and some visual transpositions that have featured concrete poetry and vispo (visual poetry) stylings.

[22] A. J. Carruthers, "1897 in 1981: Stéphane Mallarmé avec Christopher Brennan", in *Literary History and Avant-Garde Poetics in the Antipodes: Languages of Invention* (Edinburgh: Edinburgh Critical Studies in Avant-Garde Writing, Edinburgh University Press, 2024), 81.

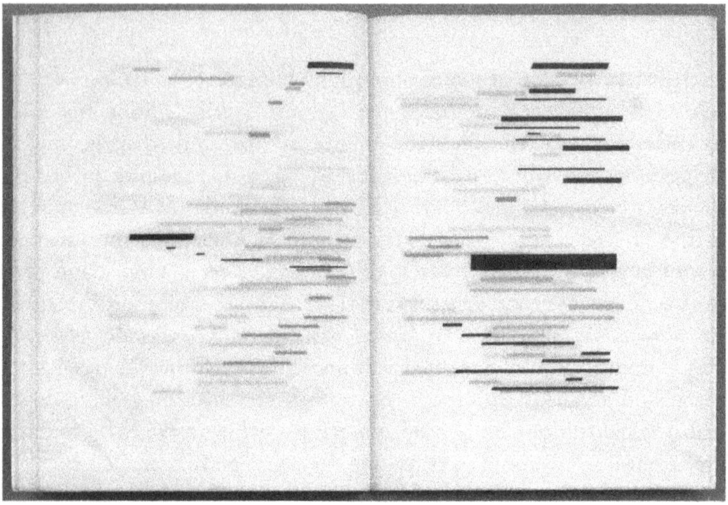

Fig. 4. A double-page spread from Broodthaers' *Un Coup de dés* (lithograph on transparent paper).

or

Late in the twentieth century and into the twenty-first, poets have unearthed, or chanced upon, new horizons in *Un Coup de dés* through parody and the kaleidoscopic linguistic possibilities of mistranslation, an approach the Oulipo movement had previously explored to great effect on various pre-texts in the second half of the twentieth century.[23] In 1998, Jim Clinefelter composed *A Throw of the Snore Will Surge the Potatoes: John M. Bennett meets Stéphane Mallarmé* on a borrowed Macintosh SE. Clinefelter's text, which draws on Bennett's rowdy poems and intersperses clip art from a reprint of an early Sears Roebuck Catalogue, pokes fun at Mallarmé's obsession with sonority and his cryptic lines that have challenged readers and translators alike—"*LE MAÎTRE surgi inférant de cette conflagration à ses pieds de l'horizon unanime que se prépare s'agite et mêle au poing qui l'étreindrait* in the original, becomes: "THE MASTER

[23] See Harry Mathews, 'Translation and the Oulipo: The Case of the Persevering Maltese', *Electronic Book Review*, March 1, 1997, https://electronicbookreview.com/essay/translation-and-the-oulipo-the-case-of-the-persevering-maltese/.

knees inferring from this conflagration drips there as soft threatens the unique clam".[24]

aussi

In 2006, Rachel Blau DuPlessis penned a sometimes cheeky, sometimes homophonic version of *Un coup de dés*, 'Draft 73: Vertigo', whose linguistic antics burlesque Mallarmé's fetish for blank space and the void through "penetration and/ or fellation of vanishing points". The poem features some typographical play, use of page space via terraced stanzas and three large child-written letters (that evoke calligraphy), although it doesn't mimic Mallarmé's full use of the double-page spread. Her chapbook *POESIS*, from 2016, does use the same typographical and page structure, and is a heightened intellectual interrogation of language, signification and its impossibilities—it "cannot 'contain' any of this // but // poesis might"[25]—however it is not a homophonic translation, nor a mistranslation, but rather an extrapolation of and adaptation of Mallarméan themes into Blau DuPlessis's sustained interest in the limits of language in poetic praxis.

aussi

It is notable that DuPlessis's *POESIS* was first published by an Australian: expat poet, author and scholar Louis Armand selected the poem to appear in the fifth issue of his radical poetics journal *VLAK*, based in Prague.[26]

or

The first fully homophonic translation of *Un Coup de dés*, titled *A Fluke: A mistranslation of Stéphane Mallarmé's "Un coup de dés..." with parallel French pretext*, was rather conjured by Australian poet Chris Edwards in 2005, and its renegade inversion of the French is indicative of the peculiar fascination that Australian poets in particular seem to have for Mallarmé and *Un Coup de dés*, and for turning the language of colonial forebears

[24] Jim Clinefelter, *A Throw of the Snore Will Surge the Potatoes: John M. Bennett meets Stéphane Mallarmé* (Columbus, Ohio: Luna Bisonte Productions, 1998), n.p.

[25] Rachel Blau DuPlessis, *POESIS* (Houston, Texas: Little Red Leaves Textile Series, 2016), n.p.

[26] See Louis Armand, ed., *VLAK* 5 (2015): 329–49.

Down Under, or antipodal (diametrically opposed), and this fascination can be traced all the way back to the year that Mallarmé's gnomic poem first appeared.

or

"Shipwrecked on the shoals of contingency"[27]—poets in so-called Australia seem particularly haunted by this poem, not just by Mallarmé the aesthete.[28] Its publication in *Cosmopolis* in Paris in 1897 struck a nerve or, rather, a vessel within antipodean bloodlines, starting with Christopher Brennan, who was the first, and quickest, in the world to take up Mallarmé's provocations. *Un Coup de dés* was the score that inspired him to compose "Musicopoematographoscope", also in 1897, a large handwritten *mimique* manuscript, or pastiche, that transposed the more extreme aesthetics of an avant-garde French Symbolism into the settler Australian poetic psyche (though it languished in manuscript form until it was finally published in 1981). Now well into the twenty-first century, *Un Coup de dés* is still a blueprint for experimentation Down Under, spawning two homophonic mistranslations—the aforementioned "A Fluke" (2005) by Chris Edwards and "Desmond's Coupé" (2006) by John Tranter—both revelling/rebelling in the abject, and in "errors and wrecks". The following subchapters will provide a comparative reading of these homophonic bedfellows, trace their relation(ship)s to their antecedents in Mallarmé and Brennan, and will then divagate into

27 Weinfield, "Commentary", 266.

28 The Australian attention to Mallarmé is a longstanding one. Christopher Brennan imported French Symbolism into Australian poetry through his own imitative style after first reading Mallarmé in 1893 while in Berlin. Australian literary editors such as A. G. Stephens expanded Mallarmé's influence, which in turn influenced the work of most major twentieth-century Australian poets. For a comprehensive tracing of this history, see John Hawke, *Australian Literature and the Symbolist Movement* (Wollongong: University of Wollongong Press, 2009). Prior to this monograph, Australian academic and teacher of French at University of Melbourne, Jill Anderson, edited a significant internationalist anthology of essays: *Australian Divagations: Mallarmé & the 20th Century* (New York: Peter Lang Publishing, 2002). Among other things, this anthology also covers Mallarmé's influence on late twentieth-century Australian poets John Forbes, David Brooks, Chris Wallace-Crabbe and Kevin Hart. New generations of Australian scholars have continued this tradition: see Robert Boncardo and Christian R. Gelder, *Mallarmé: Rancière, Milner, Badiou* (Lanham: Rowman & Littlefield, 2018) and Boncardo, *Mallarmé and the Politics of Literature: Sartre, Kristeva, Badiou, Rancière* (Edinburgh: Edinburgh University Press, 2019).

various theories of translation and punning to open up the valencies of mistranslation, before considering its implications in the settler Australian poetry context.

2

In his reluctant introduction to *Un Coup de dés* (he only wrote it to appease the wishes of the periodical *Cosmopolis*), Mallarmé "retain[s] a religious veneration" for "the ancient technique of verse", to which he "attribute[s] the empire of passion and of dreams".[29] He may well have been attempting to appease traditional readers, but at the same time Mallarmé is alluding to a crisis which, at first, plays out as a revolution in French prosody, but "is not merely a crisis *of* poetry or verse, but a crisis of modernity—indeed, a religious crisis that manifests itself *in* poetry or verse".[30] Furthermore, in his famous essay *Crise de vers* Mallarmé struggles with the admission that "Languages [are] imperfect insofar as they are many; the absolute one is lacking … the diversity, on earth, of idioms prevents anyone from proffering words that would otherwise be, when made uniquely, the material truth. This prohibition is explicitly devastating, in Nature … where nothing leads one to take oneself for God".[31]

He demonstrates that languages are at once imperfect and multiple, that there is no necessary or natural connection between word and thing, between sound and sense, offering the example that *jour* (day), for instance, is a dark sound while *nuit* (night) is a bright sound. This is the same as Ferdinand de Saussure's revolutionary formulation—that the relationship between the linguistic signifier and what it signifies is arbitrary,[32] which suggests that Mallarmé's crisis was also a crisis between subject and object, and which could explain how he came to a poetics of indecision, polyphony and counterpoint. Adorno had similar aesthetic concerns when he wrote of the subject-object bind:

29 Mallarmé, *Collected Poems*, 123.

30 Weinfield, "'Thinking out afresh the whole poetic problem': Brennan's Prescience; Mallarmé's Accomplishment", *Southerly* 68.3 (2008): 11.

31 Mallarmé, "Crisis of Verse", 205.

32 Ferdinand de Saussure, *Course in General Linguistics*, 1893, trans. Wade Baskin (New York: Columbia University Press, 2011), 67–70.

> In the artwork the subject is neither the observer nor the creator nor absolute spirit, but rather spirit bound up with, performed and mediated by the object.
>
> For the artwork and thus for its theory, subject and object are its own proper elements and they are dialectical in such a fashion that whatever the work is composed of—material, expression, and form—is always both.[33]

aussi

Jacques Derrida describes Mallarmé's poetics as "and/or", citing Mallarmé's deft use of homonyms and puns and their chain-like linkages across his oeuvre not as a crisis but as the key to its understanding, and to new possibilities for literature:

> Let us not forget that these chains, which are infinitely vaster, more powerful and intertwined than is even possible to hint at here, are as if without support, always suspended. It is the Mallarméan doctrine of *suggestion*, of undecided allusion. Such indecision, which enables them to move alone and without end, cuts them off, in spite of appearances, from all meaning (signified theme) and from all referents (the thing itself, and the conscious or unconscious intention of the author). Which leads to numerous traps for criticism, and numerous new procedures and categories to be invented.[34]

or

Weinfield describes Mallarmé's chains with an almost religious fervour, even as he acknowledges the immanence of words and things:

> polysyllabic chains of homophonic rhymes, rhymes that will hyperbolically, but also actually, evoke the island of poetry from which the spirit has been exiled and in which it can dwell …
>
> For the inhabitants of Mallarmé's mythical island, subject-object distinctions and discrepancies between words and things no longer obtain. Everything is immanent and no longer transcendent;

33 Theodor W. Adorno, "Subject-Object", 226–7.

34 Derrida, "Mallarmé", 120–1.

> everything comes immediately to the eye, to sight itself, and so there is no longer any need for the visionary.[35]

aussi

Regarding Derrida's "doctrine of suggestion, and undecided allusion", there is a little-known theory of anagrams that Saussure worked on in his many unpublished notebooks. Tracing the works of Homer and others to discover laws governing the distribution of consonants and vowels, Saussure accidentally noticed recurrent groups of phonemes that combined to form prolonged echoes of words of special import—hidden motivic theme-words embedded in poetic texts. Jean Starobinski, in unearthing these unfinished theories, enters into conversation with Saussure's notes and addresses some unanswered questions of the origin or function of the anagram-forming process. Applying a Claude Lévi-Strauss phrase, "phonic tinkering", he aligns Saussure's process with a poet's, and describes the poem in general as an emanation—an "act of words" [fait de parole] which "appears as the superfluous luxury of the hypogram" (the hypogram being the semantic nucleus of a poem, whether a title or motivic theme-word). One of the key conclusions Starobinski comes to is that "the words of a work are rooted in other, antecedent words, and that they are not directly chosen by the formative consciousness."[36] In other words, the poetic process, however procedural, is largely unconscious—words are written one by one, yet patterns of words upon words form subliminally. Starobinski continues: "To the question What lies beneath the line? the answer is not the creative subject but the inductive word. Not that Ferdinand de Saussure goes so far as to erase the role of artistic subjectivity, but it does seem to him that this subjectivity can produce its text only by passage through a pre-text".[37]

35 Weinfield, "'Thinking out afresh the whole poetic problem'", 21.

36 Jean Starobinski, *Words Upon Words: The Anagrams of Ferdinand Saussure*, 1971, trans. Olivia Emmet (New Haven: Yale University Press, 1979), 120–1.

37 Jean Starobinski, *Words Upon Words*, 121.

or

As Julia Kristeva has written: "every text is from the outset under the jurisdiction of other discourses which impose a universe on it".[38] Kristeva argues that "any text is constructed as a mosaic of quotations; any text is the absorption and transformation of another. The notion of intertextuality replaces that of intersubjectivity, and poetic language is read as at least double".[39]

or

Putting it another way, Roland Barthes wrote: "We know now that a text is not a line of words releasing a single 'theological' meaning (the 'message' of the AuthorGod) but a multidimensional space in which a variety of writings, none of them original, blend and clash. The text is a tissue of quotations drawn from the innumerable centres of culture".[40]

aussi

Saussure and Starobinski's theory of anagrams need not only be applied to Mallarmé's *Un Coup de dés*. Derrida focuses on the expansive use of the word *or* throughout Mallarmé's oeuvre as an example of his punning chains (*or* is just one of many words employed in this manner). As suggested previously, *or* isn't stable as a word. It's a noun ("gold"), an adjective ("golden"), and a conjunction ("now"), and its English homonyn "or" is a conjunction that links alternatives, giving the "otherwise" equal billing. Mallarmé utilises the sound and meaning of *or*, not just as a word on its own, but within words, and amongst many other similar concatenations, to redouble semantic indecision and scatter meaning: "no identity is stable enough, of itself, to give rise to relationships of the

[38] Julia Kristeva, in Jonathan Culler, *The Pursuit of Signs: Semiotics, Literature, Deconstruction*, (London: Routledge & Kegan Paul, 1981), 105.

[39] Saussure's anagrams are a ghostly kind of intertextuality, a term associated with poststructural theorists that refers to more than just the "influences" of writers on each other. Julia Kristeva coined this semiotic notion, proposing that language has powers which not only exceed individual control but also determine subjectivity. Kristeva, *The Kristeva Reader*, ed. Toril Moi (New York: Columbia University Press, 1986), 37.

[40] Roland Barthes, *Image-Music-Text*, trans. Stephen Heath (London: Fontana, 1977), 146.

whole and the part, of cause and effect".[41] Derrida then shows how, in a single line from Mallarmé's *Les mots anglais*, we can gain a taste for how the word *or* and its multiplicity might concatenate across an oeuvre: "*une eclipse, or, telle est l'heure*", which translates in one sense as "an eclipse, now, such is the hour". The other meanings of gold, goldenness, money, seasonality, midnight, time, epoch, are all at once there in the French. In this golden light, the fragmentation that is so indicative of modern poetry under the modern subject might be seen as refractions of the *word* that Mallarmé has "by disintegration, liberated".[42] And so, if we now apply to Mallarmé's line an extreme translation (a mistranslation at the level of letter and word, swerving as one may) using an Australian vernacular, we might get: "An eclipse! Gold! Such is life!" Or homophonically: "You kleptos all tell a lie".

aussi

So what is mistranslation? According to the Oxford English Dictionary, to mistranslate is to translate (something) incorrectly: "passages from the Bible were either mistranslated or taken out of context".[43]

or

"Take a poem, or part of a poem, in a foreign language and translate it word for word according to what it sounds like in English … Try this with a language you know and then with one you don't know. Don't use a dictionary, just rely on what your ears hear and go from there … Use slang and other nonstandard English words. Let the syntax take care of itself."[44]

aussi

Mistranslation in poetry, according to many experimenting or procedural poets—as in Charles Bernstein's instructions above for a homophonic translation—is a means to an end, a constraint-based, generative practice,

[41] Derrida, "Mallarmé", 124–5.

[42] Derrida, "Mallarmé", 116.

[43] *Oxford English Dictionary*.

[44] Charles Bernstein, "Homophonic Translation", in *The Practice of Poetry: Writing Exercises from Poets Who Teach*, ed. Robin Behn and Twichell Chase (New York: Harper, 1992), 126.

whereby a poet "translates" another poem (usually from a foreign language) into something *newly mistaken*. Transposition from one mode to another, as a practice/praxis, short-circuits control, bringing chance to the fore—the poet is at the whim of words and their swervings. To double-up (or double-down) on Walter Benjamin's "Translation is a mode", let's think of mistranslation—predicated on ceding the initiative to a pre-text—as a *mood* "in which meaning has ceased to be the watershed for the flow of language and the flow of revelation".[45]

aussi

Gérard Genette, in his seminal book on parody and the manifold relationships a text may have with prior texts, *Palimpsests: Literature in the Second Degree*, offers a surprising prototype for the genre of homophonic translation: *Mots d'Heures: Gousses, Rames* by Louis d'Antin van Rooten (1967), a series of French transphonations of *Mother Goose Rhymes*:

Humpty Dumpty	Un petit d'un petit	A little one of a little one
Sat on a wall.	S'étonne aux Halles	Was surprised at the Market
Humpty Dumpty	Un petit d'un petit	A little one of a little one
Had a great fall.	Ah! degrés te fallent	Oh, degrees fail you!
All the king's horses	Indolent qui ne sort cesse	Lazy is he who leaves stops
And all the king's men	Indolent qui ne se mène	Lazy is he who is not led
Couldn't put Humpty	Qu'importe un petit	Who cares about a little one
Together again.	Tout gai de Reguennes.	All happy with Reguennes[46]

or

One of the classic avant-garde contemporary examples of homophonic translation is the Zukofskys' *Catullus* (1969), in which Celia and Louis Zukofsky take a visceral approach to the material surface of the original Latin of Catullus' poetry—its shape, sound, and rhythm—and translate it into English by trying "to breathe / the 'literal' meaning with him" (note the quotations around "literal", as if to redefine it).[47] They dismantle

[45] Walter Benjamin, "The Task of the Translator", in *Illuminations*, 1955, trans. Harry Zohn, 1968 (London: Fontana, 1992), 71 and 82.

[46] Gérard Genette, *Palimpsests: Literature in the Second Degree*, 1982, trans. Channa Newman and Claude Doubinsky (Lincoln: University of Nebraska Press, 1997), 41.

[47] Celia Thaew Zukofsky and Louis Zukofsky, *Catullus* [*Gai Valeri Catulli Veronensis Liber*] (London: Cape Golliard, 1969), not paginated.

the concept of transparent literalism (the dominant mode of most translations) and at the same time redefine semantic correspondence.[48] In poem #22, Catullus ridicules a fellow poet for insisting on new papyrus for his prolific but poor verse, instead of using the cheaper palimpsest:

> idemque longe plurimos facit uersus.
> puto esse ego illi milia aut decem aut plura
> perscripta, nec sic ut fit in palimpsesto
> relata: cartae regiae, noui libri,
> noui umbilici, lora rubra membranae,
> derecta plumbo et pumice omnia aequata[49]

The Zukovskys translate this like so:

> his damn cue's long reams of preoccupied verses.
> Put his goal at ten thousand, some decked out plural.
> Poor script, eh? not so it fit incest in palimpsest—
> realloted: quires, regal eye, new cylinders,
> new little umbiliform roll ends, rubric lore, thongs,
> membranes ruled plumb o (my) all equated with pumice.[50]

Josef Horáček describes the Zukofskys' approach: "Syntax breaks up considerably, with phrases sliding from one to the next without precise boundaries; certain words could be read variably as part of two adjoining phrases. Vocabulary now oscillates freely from archaic to mundane to bawdy: the distinctions among different levels of diction are effectively erased. Semantic correspondence is fully subordinated to homophony but not in the least ignored."[51]

[48] Josef Horáček, "Pedantry and Play: The Zukofsky *Catullus*", *Comparative Literature Studies* 51.1 (2014): 106.

[49] Gaius Valerius Catullus, *The Poems of Catullus: A Bilingual Edition*, trans. Peter Green (Berkeley: University of California Press, 2007), 66.

[50] Zukofsky and Zukofsky, *Catullus*, not paginated.

[51] Horáček, "Pedantry and Play", 114.

or

Mistranslation can be seen as any of these: "word writing",[52] palimpsest, a doubling, a mirroring, a homage, a parody, high jinks, a remix of a classic score, or a combination of these. There is always a trace of the original, however far a mistranslation departs, so it could also be seen as a ghosting or a haunting—as in, the haunting of a location. Whatever the preferred method, whether loose or "pedantic", this "witty translation game"[53] requires alternative ways of reading, and/or other interpretive approaches.

aussi

"Mallarmé does not belong completely to French literature", writes Derrida. His "*or*-play" is "a brilliant demonstration of a recourse to the homonym, to what Aristotle denounced as bad poetry, as an instrument of rhetoric for sophists". Having "broken with the protocols of rhetoric", his poetry "escapes the control of [muted classical and philosophical] representation … demonstrates *in practice* its nonpertinence", and makes him at once a sophist and an outlaw of Plato.[54]

or

A cast out. Which could be one reason why *Un Coup de dés* has spawned a number of mirror images, or mistranslations, Down Under—it resonates with settler Australian sensibilities of the outsider or the reject. Former prime minister Paul Keating was criticised in 1994 for calling Australia "the arse end of the world",[55] and yet his suggestion that the hard-done-by outsider sensibility is a national preoccupation, evoking as he did its convict history, isn't unfounded. In saying so, Keating also perpetuated, however obliquely, the idea of Atlantis that Plato perpetuated—that

52 Charles Olson, "Logography", in *Additional Prose: A Bibliography on America, Proprioception & Other Notes & Essays*, ed. George F. Butterick (Bolinas: Four Seasons Foundation, 1974), 20.

53 Horáček, "Pedantry and Play: The Zukofsky *Catullus*", 108.

54 Derrida, "Mallarmé", 121–6.

55 Paul Keating, in Robert Milliken, "Keating's rear view of the lucky country causes storm: Careless remarks have damaged the PM's nationalist stance", *Independent*, June 27, 1994, http://www.independent.co.uk/news/world/keatings-rear-view-of-the-lucky-country-causes-storm-careless-remarks-have-damaged-the-pms-1425378.html.

this huge island continent was located somewhere on the opposite, underside of the world (*antipodes*, originally from Greek, means "having the feet opposite", which chimes neatly with mistranslation's tendency to undermine the foot or feet of a poem). Taking place at the bottom of a shipwreck, *Un Coup de dés* resonates because of its preoccupation with the impossibility of *under*standing existence.

or

Troubled by the flipped hemisphere, or just troubling away at their misappropriations of *Un Coup de dés*, Australian poets might otherwise see their work as a kind of "understumbling", to pinch a word from Jacques Lacan, who in turn nicked the word from a slang dictionary for his lecture on anxiety.[56]

or

Sidere Mens Eadem Mutato: "The constellation is changed, the disposition is the same" / "The same minds under different stars", which is also, oddly enough, the motto of the University of Sydney, where Christopher Brennan, the subject of the next subchapter, was a Professor, and from where he was, quite literally, cast out.[57]

[56] Jacques Lacan, 2004, *Anxiety: The Seminar of Jacques Lacan Book X*, ed. Jacques Alain-Miller, trans. A. R. Price (Cambridge: Polity Press, 2014).

[57] See Lionel Lindsay, "Christopher Brennan lost his post at Sydney University through drink and an adventure", *News*, Adelaide, December 3, 1954, https://trove.nla.gov.au/newspaper/article/131218020.

3

In the latter part of the nineteenth century, Mallarmé's poetics greatly influenced the work of the young Australian poet Christopher Brennan, whose formal variations of the *Symboliste* style have since defined his oeuvre.[58] The work of Brennan's that is often overlooked, however, or thought of as an anomaly, is his handwritten *Prose-Verse-Poster-Algebraic-Symbolico-Riddle Musicopoematographoscope & Pocket Musicopoematographoscope*, a large facsimile of two poems that mimic the appearance of Mallarmé's *Un Coup de dés*, and that were composed in the same year, 1897, but lay dormant and subterranean until formally published in 1981, nearly 50 years after his death. The central poem, "Musicopoematographoscope", spaced across the page like *Un Coup de dés*, but not utilising the gutter and double-page spread as syntactic Abyss, is an immediate "in" version—a version meaningful (which is significant) only to the cognoscenti (the "in" crowd). In this case, this consisted of two people, Brennan himself and Dowell O'Reilly, Labor member for Parramatta, who was Brennan's closest friend and for many years the poem's only reader. O'Reilly had "attacked" Brennan's normative *Symboliste* verses for their "obscurity" and claimed that his poetry should appeal to public readerships.[59] John Tranter, in his 1982 *Sydney Morning Herald* review of *Prose-Verse-Poster-Algebraic-Symbolico-Riddle Musicopoematographoscope & Pocket Musicopoematographoscope*

[58] *Poems 1913*, for instance, is a transplantation of and homage to the more formal *Symboliste* aesthetics; it is an oeuvre whose *écume* came to haunt Australian poetry, in part because its obscurity both baffled reviewers and became exemplary for other poets: Brennan was the first of waves of poets, including Judith Wright, John Shaw Nielsen, Gwen Harwood, A. D. Hope, James McAuley, and Kenneth Slessor, among others, who transposed a Symbolist, European-influenced literary modernism on to Australia's shores in the first half of the twentieth century. In the latter half of the century, the significance of these poets and their lineage came to be taught and studied first, and predominantly, at the University of Sydney. From the early 1990s until 2012, the University of Sydney dedicated an entire Honours English unit to the influence of French Symbolism on Australian poets.

[59] Axel Clark, quoted in Michael Farrell, *Writing Australian Unsettlement: Modes of Poetic Invention 1796-1945* (New York: Palgrave MacMillan, 2015), 140.

recounts Brennan's stab at his reviewers and condemns it: "The main burden of its complaint can be traced by following through the poem the words in large capitals: 'I DON'T GIVE A TINKER'S DAMN FOR THE PUBLIC AND THEY RETURN THE COMPLIMENT'."[60]

aussi

Michael Farrell adds that, in "Reviewing Brennan's belated publication … Tranter suggests that it was 'probably the first ever parody of free verse in the history of English literature'. We can imagine a minor poetics history of Australian poets parodying things first before taking them seriously: understanding through parody perhaps."[61] Understumbling much.

or

In large capital letters, the "I DON'T GIVE A TINKER'S DAMN…" sentence, spaced out through the double-page spreads, echoes the style of the embedded and elongated title of *UN COUP DE DÉS JAMAIS N'ABOLIRA LE HASARD*, fragmented as it is, but not its IDEA. Not necessarily aiming to "translate" Mallarmé's "and/or" poetics, in needling his critics Brennan rather self-consciously sticks to the letter of the "law of correspondences", the straighter and more canonical *Symboliste* conception that poetry be an evocative network of symbolic associations:

> O that I grant you // being / existent / undeniable / irreducible // in all heaviness / immovable / without wings / a brick [62]

[60] John Tranter, 1982, "Brennan's Tinker's damn", review of *Prose-Verse-Poster-Algebraic-Symbolico-Riddle Musicopoematographoscope & Pocket Musicopoematographoscope* by Christopher Brennan, *Jacket* 29, April 2006 (originally published in the *Sydney Morning Herald*), http://johntranter.com/reviewer/1982-brennan-oscope.shtml.

[61] Michael Farrell, "Rebellious Tropes: Michael Farrell on Toby Fitch", review of *Where Only the Sky had Hung Before* in *Sydney Review of Books*, May 2020, https://sydneyreviewofbooks.com/reviews/rebellious-tropes.

[62] Christopher Brennan, "Musicopoematographoscope", *Prose-Verse-Poster-Algebraic-Symbolico-Riddle Musicopoematographoscope & Pocket Musicopoematographoscope* (Erskineville: Hale & Iremonger, 1981), 21.

a phrase which evokes Charles Baudelaire's albatross,[63] itself used to symbolise the poet burdened with fate and semantics (the albatross's brutal mistreatment at the hands of sailors is a metaphor for the poet's plight in a society that fails to understand them), while subverting that imagery by transmuting said bird(s) ("without wings") into a singular symbol of labour ("a brick") that could be read in a number of ways, but the obvious way would be that Brennan's readers are thick, as dumb as a brick, and hence unable to see, nor hear and so fly. Later, he flat-out pans his critics in a heavy Aussie drawl:

> THEY // Bentley's bungler's / from the leather & duft / I long ago renounced / hither rush / hawklike / their claws / & dirty their noses[64]

or

Occasionally, "Musicopoematographoscope" toys with, or rather breaks the toy of, Mallarmé's "and/or" poetics. And this is where his poem becomes exciting. On the title poster page, Brennan mocks Mallarmé with a punning Australian vernacular: "MAISONG", "PAREE", and "MALAHRRMAY".[65] Here, Brennan also mocks himself and his imitative, parodic translation—his poetic dalliance, or liaison, with the French—bringing to mind Judith Butler's writings on drag: "In imitating gender, drag implicitly reveals the imitative structure of gender itself—as well as its contingency."[66] If we think of translation as drag—of the poet pretending to be another, of how a translation is ostensibly one language system imitating another—it reveals the imitative structure of language itself, and by extension its ability to queer, to be queer, and susceptibility to being queered.

63 See Charles Baudelaire, *L'Albatros*, 1859.

64 Brennan, "Musicopoematographoscope", 17.

65 Brennan, "Musicopoematographoscope", 9.

66 Judith Butler, *Gender Trouble: Feminism and the Subversion of Identity* (New York: Routledge, 1990), 137.

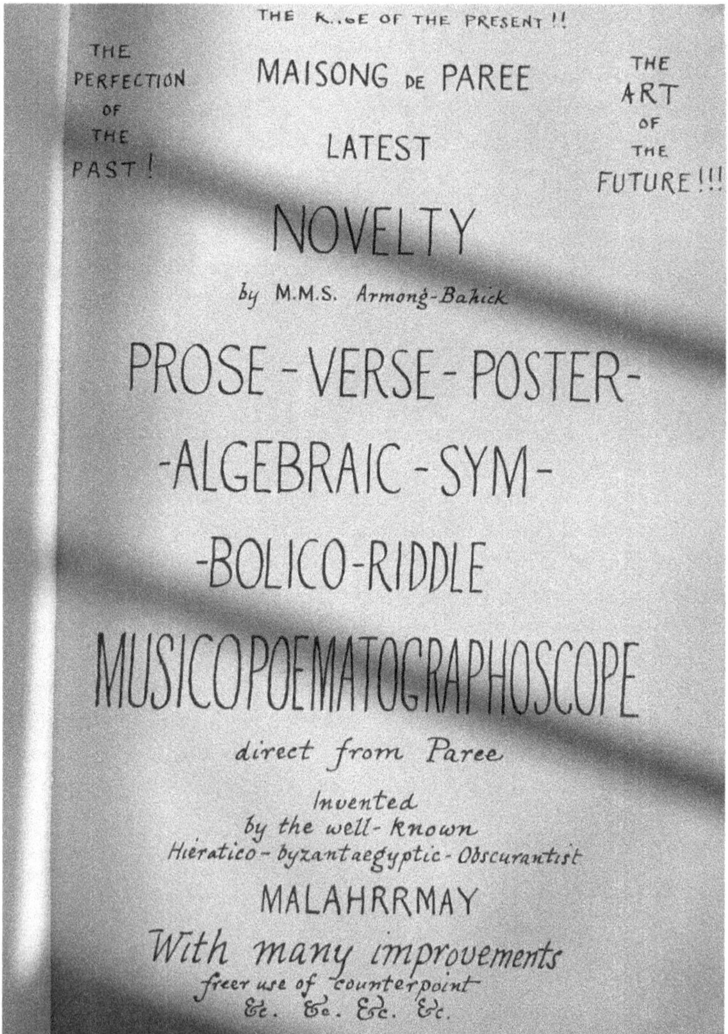

Fig. 5. The title page of Christopher Brennan's *Prose-Verse-Poster-Algebraic-Symbolico-Riddle Musicopoematographoscope* (1981).

aussi

Other moments of mistranslation occur, or can be seen to occur, perhaps laterally, as fragments seem cherrypicked from the original French and are half-translated, with a hint of homophony: "… *le temps de souffleter* …" ["at the moment (or time) of striking"] could well have been the prompt for "THIS TIME BUT AGHOST", which has been read by Australian scholar-poet A. J. Carruthers as a prescient Brennan foreshadowing the general belatedness of the avant-garde in Australia ("the day may never come; an avant-garde procrastinates, its age has not been appointed by History"), since the publication of "Musicopoematographoscope" in 1981 is prototypical of such belatedness across other literary avant-garde movements Down Under. Carruthers asserts: "its contemporaneity is an anticipatory critique of Antipodal belatedness".[67] Perhaps Brennan wasn't just "aghast" at his critics but also *struck* by his pre-avant-garde-ness.

aussi

Are these instances of mistranslation a transnational echo or a wild colonial (mis)appropriation? Michael Farrell has described it as a work of "unsettlement", that it "unsettles Brennan's own canon",[68] the historical emergence of Modernism too (it was an early instance of modernist collage), and therefore unsettles the *Symboliste* legacy in Australia as it has come to be known.

or

Kate Fagan, in an essay on Chris Edwards (whose misappropriation of Mallarmé will be discussed in the next subchapter), describes Brennan's poem's "maverick flamboyance … its feral nature" as effecting "a kind of satirical distance from anxious Anglo-colonial readings that might relegate Australian literature to a second rung after transplanted European models", and as suggestive of "a deeper unease about the legitimacy of antipodean takes on cultural internationalism", citing John Hawke's

[67] Carruthers, "1897 in 1981: Stéphane Mallarmé avec Christopher Brennan", 65–70.

[68] Michael Farrell, *Writing Australian Unsettlement: Modes of Poetic Invention 1796-1945* (New York: Palgrave MacMillan, 2015), 140–42.

Australian Literature and the Symbolist Movement, and placing Brennan at the avant-garde of this lineage:

> Hawke has argued persuasively that in the late nineteenth century "there was a stronger interest in Mallarmé's poetic philosophy in Australia than virtually anywhere else in the English-speaking world". Brennan's surrealistic description of Mallarmé as a "Hieratico-byzantaegyptic-Obscurantist" hints at a specialised reading of Mallarmé's centrality to the emergence of poetic Symbolism, while its maverick flamboyance—or perhaps its feral nature—suggests a deeper unease about the legitimacy of antipodean takes on cultural internationalism. There is a finely nuanced critique to unwrap here about late nineteenth and early twentieth century colonial Australia on the cusp of modernism, and the larger-than-life or monstrous artistic objects generated over subsequent decades by that tension—including for example the poems of Ern Malley, and more perversely, the Jindyworobak Movement. For now, I simply want to propose that "innovation" in non-Indigenous Australian poetry is marked historically by strong international identifications and sporadic refusals, and to observe that the twentieth century manifestations of these dialogues are strikingly evident in the avant-garde (or post^{n}-avant-garde) alignments of Chris Edwards' poetry.[69]

aussi

Stephanie Guest, citing Walter Benjamin, describes Brennan's poem as both an "abundant flowering" of Mallarmé's eternal yet "ever elusive text", as well as an "abundant de-flowering".[70] Illicit, it is at once a version and an inversion (a "sporadic refusal"). One could say it's also about aversion, as diversion—there is a reluctance to fully explode into the potentiality of the semantics of its Mallarméan experimentation and rather a preference to *re*vert to misgivings about his straighter verse not quite gaining the recognition he felt it deserved. However, its deviation, or deviance, does recall the atomic law of the clinamen.[71]

[69] Kate Fagan, "'A Fluke? [N]ever!': Reading Chris Edwards", *JASAL* 12.1 (2012): 4, http://www.nla.gov.au/ojs/index.php/jasal/article/view/2270.

[70] Stephanie Guest, "Nothing's Lost: Towards a Poetics of Transnational Unoriginality in Australian Poetry" (Honours thesis, Department of English, University of Sydney, 2013): 58.

[71] Rasula and McCaffery, *Imagining Language*, 532.

or

Brennan's phrase on the title page, "freer use of counterpoint", is indicative of the swerve his poem takes from the original. It speaks to the interplay of the two texts while parodying Mallarmé's "musical score". Moreover, its multiple inferences reveal the underlying conceit and erotics at play: "counterpoint" comes from medieval Latin *contrapunctum*, which is a melody pricked or marked over the original melody. From punctum we obviously get "to prick"; pricksongs too (music written, or noted, with dots or points); and we don't need to go much further. Ears are pricked to all the counterpricking going on.

aussi

The poem's use of form and written cursive as musical counterpoint "channels" different registers to compete against one another on the page, and thus across time (between French and multiple other languages—English, Australian-English and Celtic—between Brennan's and Mallarmé's differing avant-garde moments, and between historical, present and future avant-gardes): "It seeks a forward and backward movement in time. Brennan therefore uses various different graphological techniques of his own, writ by hand, including forward and backward slanted cursive, serif and non-serif fonts (one Celtic). It is in part a Celtification and colouration of its field of reference".[72]

[72] Carruthers, "1897 in 1981: Stéphane Mallarmé avec Christopher Brennan", 68-9.

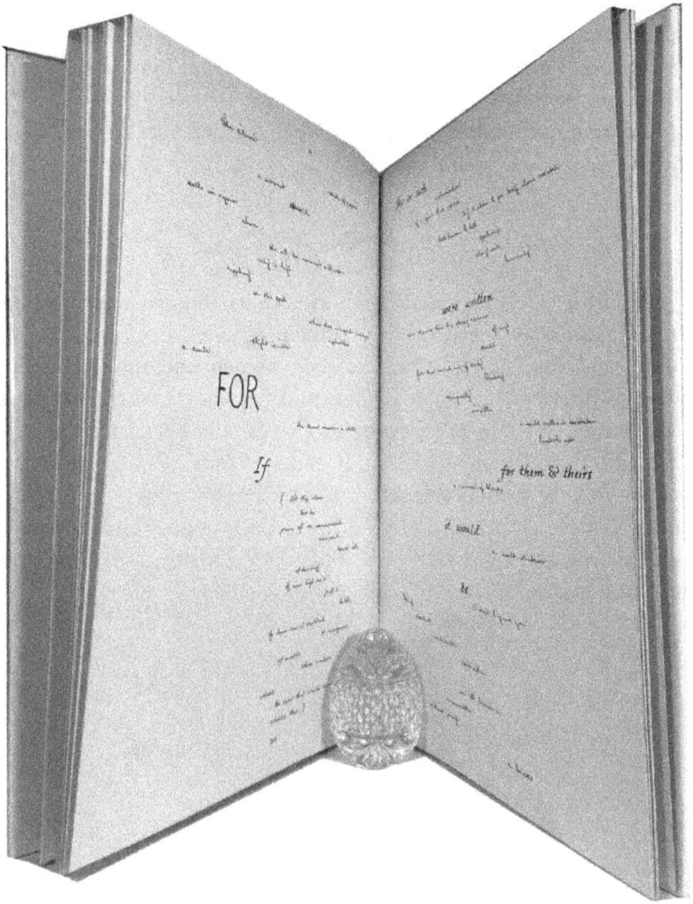

Fig. 6. A double-page spread from “Musicopoematographoscope”.

aussi

Another notable moment of linguistic intercourse comes in Brennan's final line:

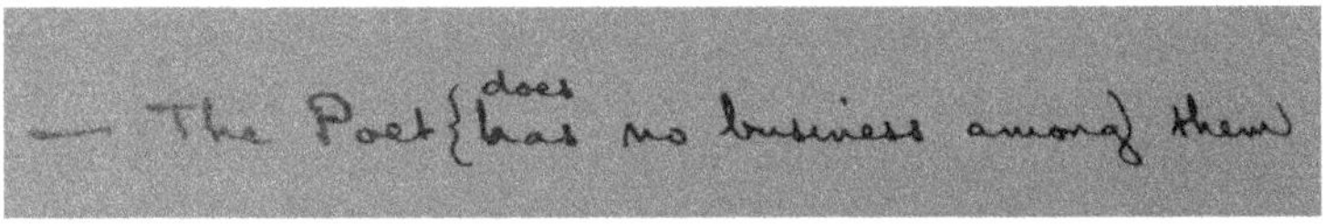

Fig. 7. The final line of "Musicopoematographoscope".

On the page, the word "does" appears just above "has" and acts as an alternative way to read the line, allows for other meanings: "does" becomes a half-pun on Mallarmé's "Dés" and the English translation "dice", and speaks to the illicit dice-play involved between a poet and their chancy, risky business with "them", their readers and critics, both among their contemporaries and subsequently across history. It summarises Brennan's grievances in one allusive/illusive line, whether he was deliberate in his use of this skewed homophone at the time or not.

or

To return to its feral nature, if we adopt Michael Farrell's reading (and unsettling) of "Musicopoematographoscope" as a biodiverse assemblage of different forms (its title page acting as a "poster" poem; its main poem "radially" dispersing its handwritten fragments across the fields of pages; its shorter poem in the same style, "Pocket Musicopoematographoscope"; its collage section, "Notices", which consists of highly punctuated quotes appropriated from various negative reviews of his poetry; the Mallarméan "silence" or "DAM wall" (with the "N" of "DAMN" negated) of the blank page 9; and its general proliferations and abundances—"&c. &c. &c. &c."),[73] then one can read the poem's manifold griping as "tinkering" with, as unsettling, the Australian colonial canon through a formal rather than semantic experiment borne of a mistranslational strategy (Brennan "misreads" Mallarmé to make a point to those misreading him) that assembles diverse cultural forms ("THE PERFECTION OF THE

[73] Farrell, *Writing Australian Unsettlement*, 139–52.

PAST!") into a whole monster[74] ahead of its time ("THE ART OF THE FUTURE!!!"):

> A tinker (in Mallarmé a *thinker*, Barnes 50) is a mender—but what is broken? O'Reilly might say the patience of the public. Brennan doesn't give a (tinker's) damn. It is not his job to mend the (illusory?) gap between public discourse and poetry, or poetry and money; his is rather that of the artist, the punctuator, mending the arts into a whole assemblage: PROSE-VERSE-POSTER-ALGEBRAIC-SYMBOLICO-RIDDLE-MUSICOPOEMATOGRAPHOSCOPE. The title enacts its journey to wholeness, in that the hyphens fall away at "MUSICO…" As tinker, then, Brennan can be seen to care for a wholeness of culture.[75]

or

While Brennan's tract may seem churlish, there's a nascent "and/or" poetics—an early *or*-play—at work in Australian poetry. Its larrikinism, maverick contrariness and queerness is evident in Brennan's imitative process and flamboyance. And he was very quick to pen his parody of Mallarmé; he was the first. Despite his own and ongoing Mallarméan project (that of introducing Australian poetry at large to the more traditional forms and imagery of French *Symboliste* poetry), by simultaneously and urgently rolling the dice on "Musicopoematographoscope"—his spoof pastiche that upends the very same *Symboliste* vogue—in the end Brennan presented two different, diverging options for Australian poetry just as Federation loomed in 1901, the year that established Australia officially

[74] Many moments and projects in Australian poetic history have been characterised as "monstrous". Australian poet Jaya Savige writes of silence and monsters in Australian poetry, and provides an almost exhaustive catalogue of instances—formal, imagistic, metaphorical and conceptual—including the "cannabalism" of Chris Edwards' version of *Un Coup de dés*, in 'Creation's Holiday', *Poetry Magazine*, May 2016: https://www.poetryfoundation.org/poetrymagazine/articles/89027/creations-holiday-on-silence-and-monsters-in-australian-poetry. However, he doesn't mention Brennan and his "Musicopoematographoscope", an obvious though sometimes forgotten progenitor of silence and the monstrous, perhaps because it went unpublished (silent) for so long and thus never became canon.

[75] Farrell, *Writing Australian Unsettlement*, 149. See also Katherine Barnes, "'With a smile barely wrinkling the surface': Christopher Brennan's Large Musicopoematographoscope and Mallarmé's *Un Coup de dés*", *XIX: Dix-Neuf*, Number 9 (October 2007), 44–56.

as part of the Commonwealth and a "successful" colonialist state. The former, more traditional *Symboliste* verse option, and an arguably more colonial poetics, was adopted hook, line and sinker in twentieth-century Australian poetics, while the latter and alternative (and far more playfully experimental and subversive) became a belatedly discovered shipwreck.

aussi

Over a hundred years hence, Chris Edwards and John Tranter have both written homophonic mistranslations of Mallarmé's *Un Coup de dés*. Both were published online in *Jacket* magazine[76] in 2006, though Edwards published his first in a chapbook edition by Monogene in 2005.[77] At that time, Edwards encouraged Tranter, according to Tranter writing about Tranter in the third person in his creative PhD, to also finish and publish his mistranslation as a "friendly rival".[78] The next two subchapters will compare these two homophonic bedfellows and their versions of *Un Coup de dés*.

[76] *Jacket* magazine, widely regarded as one of the first and most significant international online poetry journals, was founded in 1997 in Australia by John Tranter. It is now known as *Jacket2*, after Tranter gifted the magazine to the University of Pennsylvania in 2010.

[77] Chris Edwards, *A Fluke: A mistranslation of Stéphane Mallarmé's "Un coup de dés…" with parallel French pretext* (Thirroul: Monogene, 2005).

[78] Tranter, "Distant Voices" (Doctor of Creative Arts Thesis, School of Journalism and Creative Writing, University of Wollongong, 2009): 117, http://ro.uow.edu.au/theses/3191/.

4

Collage poet Chris Edwards, who knows all too well the connotations of that descriptor (the French verb *coller* means "to paste, stick, glue", while *collage* is French slang for an illicit sexual union), took to *Un Coup de dés* with a "willy-nilly … mish-mash of approaches" (note the self-consciously silly and phallic double entendre); or, more technically, he mistranslated it with "a variety of transformational logics", including primarily homophony, but also paranomasia, litotes, malapropism, mimicry, metonymy, and translation. Yet he sticks to many of Mallarmé's poetic principles:

> At the heart of things, at the heart of the poem, at the heart of the Idea with its double proposition, is division, according to Mallarmé: the gap, the fold, or, more famously, the Abyss … The unit of composition in *Un Coup de dés* is not the line or even the page, but the double-page spread, and the Abyss is physically embodied in the fold or gutter dead centre. It's a place the eye can't quite see into, full of stapling, stitching and gluing.[79]

aussi

Maintaining the visual form of Mallarmé's poem, Edwards' "A Fluke" is a clever and ludic mimicry that parodies Mallarmé's notion of *pure literature* at the same time as achieving a kind of pure "litter chewer", rustling and mucking about in the gutter of the double-page spread, in the gulf between the phonic and the graphic (the aural and the visual), and between itself and *Un Coup de dés*:

> Mallarmé's notorious difficulty, his untranslatability—figured, for example, in the abyss between the English translations I relied on for the sense of his poems and the mutant music I could hear in the French—inspired "A Fluke", my mistranslation of *Un Coup de dés*,

[79] Chris Edwards, "Double Talk".

> which it only now occurs to me was an attempt at pure literature, marred perhaps inevitably by its own impure thoughts. (One can only remain philosophical about it.)[80]

Edwards' mutant music, his slippage from pure to impure, his awareness and adoption of this as a philosophy, exposes the libidinous nature of such a translational project—i.e. his queering, his bending over of the original text—and thus an abject revelry in the resultant collapse of signifier and signified.

or

According to Julia Kristeva, the abject refers to the human reaction (such as horror, spasms, nausea) to a threatened breakdown in meaning caused by the loss of the distinction between subject and object, between self and other. A corpse (traumatically reminding us of our own materiality) is a prime example for what causes such a reaction; other things, however, can draw the same reaction: blood, shit, sewage, even the skin that forms on the surface of warm milk.[81]

or

Incidentally—or just dentally—Derrida compares Mallarmé's method of writing, and the form it took, to the careful cutting up and reallocating of body parts: "Mallarmé knew that his 'operation' on the word was also the dissection of a corpse; of a decomposable body each part of which could be of use elsewhere". Derrida then quotes Mallarmé from *Les mots anglais*[82]: "Related to the whole of nature and in this way coming closer to the organism that possesses life, the Word presents itself, in its vowels and its diphthongs, like a piece of flesh, and, in its consonants, like a skeletal structure difficult to

[80] Edwards, "Interview with Chris Edwards", ed. Michael Brennan, *Poetry International Web* (July 1, 2011): http://www.poetryinternationalweb.net/pi/site/cou_article/item/19012/Interview-with-Chris-Edwards/en.

[81] Julia Kristeva, *Powers of Horror: An Essay on Abjection*, 1980, trans. Leon S. Roudiez (New York: Columbia University Press, 1982), 1–3.

[82] David Brooks describes *Les mot anglais* as an "eccentric account of the strange correspondences and etymologies of English words", in Brooks, *The Sons of Clovis: Ern Malley, Adoré Floupette and a secret history of Australian Poetry* (St. Lucia: University of Queensland Press, 2011), 87.

dissect".[83] And this too might be how Edwards at times saw the poem, as a body to dissect into its many parts, as an abject provocation.

aussi

Kristeva's notion of the "abject" is in direct contrast to Lacan's "object of desire", his "*objet petit a*". The *objet petit a* allows a subject to coordinate their desires, maintaining the symbolic order of meaning and intersubjectivity, whereas the abject "is radically excluded" and rather, as Kristeva writes, "draws me toward the place where meaning collapses". Our reaction to such abject material re-charges what is essentially a pre-lingual response in us: "as in true theater, without makeup or masks, refuse and corpses *show me* what I permanently thrust aside in order to live".[84] Edwards lifts the already dismembered body parts of Mallarmé's poem from the gutters of the past and re-enlivens them, dramatises them in new gutters, for new readers. His overt and queer erotic imagery, his subjectivity and knowing self-abjection, is also designed to shock those readers expecting a "straight" translation, perhaps showing them what they have "thrust" aside. Where the French of *Un Coup de dés* has:

cette blancheur rigide

dérisoire

en opposition au ciel

trop

pour ne pas marquer

exigüment

quiconque

prince amer de l'écueil

s'en coiffe comme de l'héroïque
irrésistible mais contenu
par sa petite raison virile

en foudre[85]

[83] Derrida, "Mallarmé", 117.

[84] Julia Kristeva, *Powers of Horror*, 2–3.

[85] Mallarmé, *Collected Poems*, 136–7.

"A Fluke" reads, in Australian English:

this blank rigidity

derides

in opposition to the ceiling

tramp

porn-palmer

exegetical

cock-up

prince amid sewage

your hair-do may well be considered heroic
oh irresistible make-over
parsed by rational virility

fondler[86]

or

To quote Fagan: "In an exemplary queering of his own text, Edwards performs a drama of progenitorship by robbing 'A Fluke' of stable lines while reinstating its 'sameness' as a fair copy".[87] Note the quotation marks around "sameness" because, of course, it's not a like-for-like French-English translation and rather a corpse brought back to life, a "prince amid sewage", an "exegetical / cock-up".

In Edwards' hands (fingers, or ears), Mallarmé's full title, *UN COUP DE DÉS JAMAIS N'ABOLIRA LE HASARD*, is contorted and reassembled into, "A FLUKE? [N]EVER! NOBLE LIAR, BIO-HAZARD". The brackets around the "N" are to cover both meanings of *jamais* at once: "never" and "ever", also allowing for an echo of the "Never Never", that Australian settler version of the Abyss or void—the Outback (and its legal fiction of *terra nullius*). Edwards explains his choice of title as "the remains of a quarrel … it reminded me of the quarrel that broke out in me between various possible mistranslations at every turn of phrase."[88]

86 Edwards, "A Fluke", in *People of Earth: poems* (Marrickville: Vagabond Press, 2011), 53.
87 Fagan, "'A Fluke? [N]ever!': Reading Chris Edwards", 3.
88 Edwards, "Double Talk".

The third wheel to this quarrel is Plato, his "old quarrel" between poetry and philosophy, and his "noble lie".[89] Edwards' "fluke", an unexpected piece of good luck, speaks to Mallarmé's prismatic subdivisions of the Idea (that a throw of the dice will never abolish chance), the "noble liar" to Edwards' misreadings, and "bio-hazard" of his misrenderings. As in Mallarmé, all of Edwards' fragments that fall around the title to form the poem are deduced from the flukes laid out in this conceptually hypogrammatic title.

aussi

A "fluke" can also be a parasite, a flat fish, the triangular bits on an anchor, and anything resembling that shape, like barbs on a harpoon or the tail of a whale. These connecting flukes are Mallarméan chains, but Edwards isn't creating knock-off, fake jewelry made of flukes (however much Mallarme's *La Dernière Mode* might have something to say about the connection between fashion and poetry). Edwards' chains are the stuff of chaos.

aussi

According to Edwards, in writing "A Fluke" he was guided mainly by what he calls in his "homophonically (mis)translated" Preface, "the latent conductor unreasoning verisimilitude imposes on the text" (in Mallarmé's preface it's a *fil conducteur latent*, meaning "latent guiding thread"),[90] which alludes to (presciently, in Mallarmé's case) the strange attractors of string theory/chaos theory, a late twentieth century scientific discovery. Strange attractors make an interesting theory for mistranslation, as Edwards writes:

> An attractor is the state into which a system will eventually settle. The black holes around which galaxies cluster are examples of attractors; cultural attractors include chiefs, tribes, states and anything that gives us identity, like religion, class and world view. Strange attractors are a special class. They live in phase space, a multidimensional imaginary space in which numbers can be turned into pictures. Fractal objects,

[89] A fourth wheel might be William Butler Yeats: "We make out of the quarrel with others, rhetoric, but out of the quarrel with ourselves, poetry" (in Yeats, *Mythologies* [London: Macmillan, 1924], 331).

[90] Edwards, "A Fluke", 39.

they consist of infinite numbers of curves, surfaces or manifolds, and as their name suggests, they draw things toward them.[91]

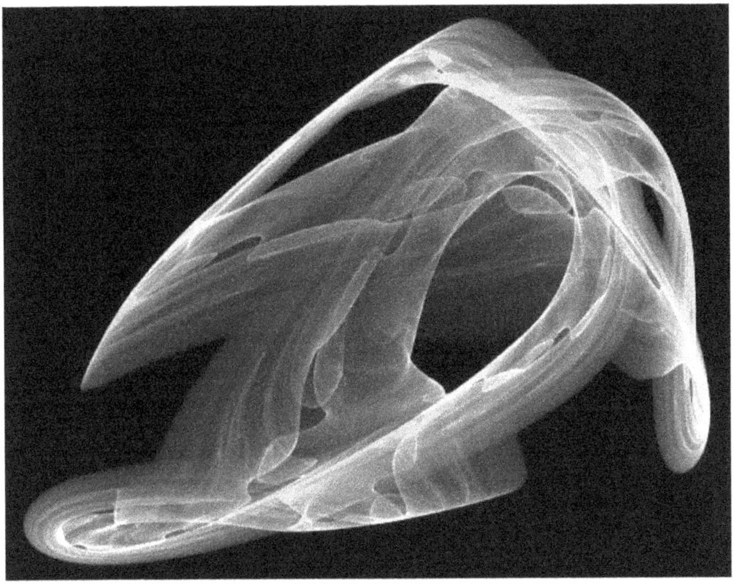

Fig. 8. Nicholas Desprez, Lorenz Attractor, *Chaoscope* (2009).

or

Mallarmé, of course, is a cultural attractor for his Australian antecedents, while *Un Coup de Dés* is the overarching strange attractor, within which many strange attractions emerge from, or occur due to its fractals.

aussi

Edwards isn't the first Australian poet to be drawn to strange attractors. Louis Armand has referred to the "sublexical 'perversions' of [James] Joyce's triads and *portmanteaux*", and to the "cyclical 'turbulence'" of the structural

[91] Edwards, "Double Talk".

schemata of *Finnegans Wake*".[92] Such perversions are not conceptually unlike Edwards' turbulent attraction to abjection, vis-à-vis mistranslation.

or

So, here, mistranslation is an abject (or per*verse*) gathering together of multiple swerving (turbulent) objects (think of Lucretius' clinamen), objects that become interchangeable (by dint of their correlations and correspondences), which brings to mind (strangely) George Bataille's *Story of the Eye*, an erotic novel that is "really the story of an object", a composition that "should be called a 'poem'", as per Roland Barthes. The initial object of attraction in the narrative is the Eye, but then other globular objects become erotically interchangeable, in both form and content: an egg (in French, egg is *oeuf* and eye is *oeil*), disc-shaped objects like a saucer of milk, then testicles. A secondary metaphorical chain concatenates from these, "made up of all the avatars of liquid: tears, milk in the cat's saucer-eye, the yolk of a soft-boiled egg, sperm and urine". At the climax of this erotic tale even the sun comes to stand in for the Eye as a "urinary liquefaction of the sky", drawing together the eye-egg-testicle metaphors.[93] Accumulated image-associations form an epic "cataract", in both senses of the word:

> by virtue of their metonymic freedom they endlessly exchange meanings and usages in such a way that breaking eggs in a bath tub, swallowing or peeling eggs (soft-boiled), cutting up or putting out an eye or using one in sex play, associating a saucer of milk with a cunt or a beam of light with a jet of urine, biting the bull's testicle like an egg or inserting it in the body—all these associations are at the same time identical and other. For the metaphor that varies them exhibits a controlled difference between them that the metonymy

[92] Louis Armand, "Constellations" in *Literate Technologies: Language, Cognition & Technics* (Prague: Litteraria Pragensia, 2006), 120. Armand has referred to strange attractors elsewhere in *Technē: James Joyce, Hypertext & Technology* (Univerzita Karlova v Praze, Nakladatelství Karolinum, 2003). He also started his introduction to the anthology *Contemporary Poetics* with an acknowledgement that "contemporary poetics" historically begins with Mallarmé: see Armand, ed., "Introduction: Transversions of the Contemporary" in *Contemporary Poetics* (Evanston: Northwestern University Press, 2007), ii–xiii.

[93] Roland Barthes, "The Metaphor of the Eye", essay in George Bataille, *Story of the Eye*, 1963, trans. Joachim Neugroschal (Harmondsworth: Penguin, 1979), 119–27.

that interchanges them immediately sets about demolishing. The world becomes *blurred*; properties are no longer separate; spilling, sobbing, urinating, ejaculating form a *wavy* meaning, and the whole of *Story of the Eye* signifies in the manner of a vibration…[94]

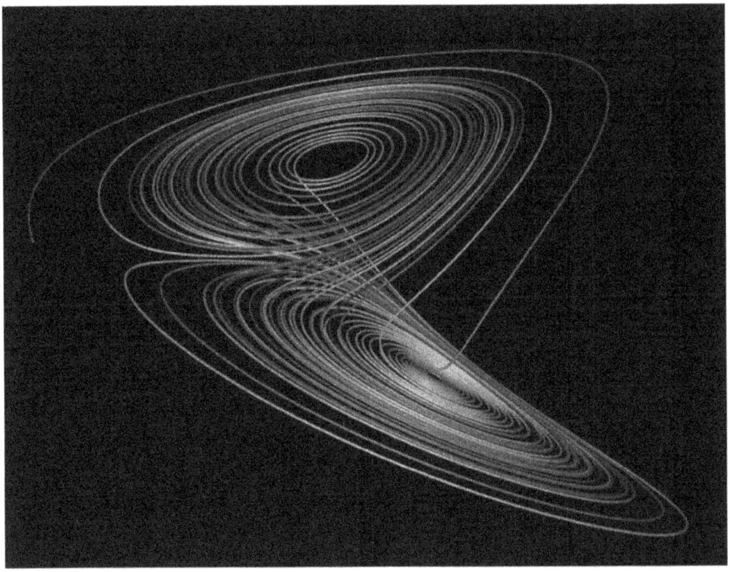

Fig. 9. Paul Bourke, Lorenz Attractor, *The Lorenz Attractor in 3D* (1997).

A homophonic translation, or simply a poem, can work as a system of attraction, of wavering objects—where the poem is not *an* object but *many* similar objects oscillating; where these word-images, these image-associations, become interchangeable—a poem in which any one of these objects could equal another. Object = desire = fetish = dream. A similar compositional approach occurs (in terms of the imagery used) in Bataille's "Solar Anus" (which Edwards quotes from in his epigraph), but let's look back to the flukes of "A Fluke", in which Edwards' word-images vibrate alongside and askew from Mallarmé's. Here's the final double-page spread (reduced in size) of these fractal objects (imagine the gutter down the middle):

[94] Barthes, "The Metaphor of the Eye", 125.

EXCEPTÉ
à l'altitude
PEUT-ÊTRE
aussi loin qu'un endroit

fusionne avec au delà

hors l'intérêt
quant à lui signalé
en général
selon telle obliquité par telle déclivité
de feux

vers
ce doit être
le Septentrion aussi Nord

UNE CONSTELLATION

froide d'oubli et de désuétude
pas tant
qu'elle n'énumère
sur quelque surface vacante et supérieure
le heurt successif
sidéralement
d'un compte total en formation

veillant
doutant
roulant
brillant et méditant

avant de s'arrêter
à quelque point dernier qui le sacre

Toute Pensée émet un Coup de Dés

Fig. 10. Final double-page spread of *Un Coup de dés*.

EXCEPT
for the attitude
MAYBE
his aussie loins proved quaintly adroit

once fused with the wrecked and disorderly
whore of the internet's
quantified signal
engendering
saloon tales obliquities and declivities
on fire

versus
say **deadhead**
less petrol oh Signor

UNCONSTITUTIONAL

fraudulent doubler of desuetude
part ant
queller of the numerous
suckers of clogged surfaces vacant and superior
each hurt succeeding
in mentioning sideways
the constantly totalled formation

veiled
doubting
roly-poly
brilliantined emetic

I want to see Rita
of the collapsible derriere oh sacred

toupéed one my little mate I guess you'll want the code word eh?

Fig. 11. Final double-page spread of "A Fluke".[95]

[95] Both figures 10 and 11 from Chris Edwards, *A Fluke: A mistranslation of Stéphane Mallarmé's "Un Coup de dés…" with parallel French pretext* (Thirroul: Monogene, 2005), not paginated.

We can read and misread many notions in Edwards' flukes here, but I want to concentrate on some of the Australian nuggets in the language for a moment:

EXCEPTÉ
à l'altitude
PEUT-ÊTRE
aussi loin qu'un endroit
fusionne avec au delà
EXCEPT
for the attitude
MAYBE
his aussie loins proved quaintly adroit
once fused with the wrecked and disorderly

Edwards uses the more colloquial "maybe" instead of "perhaps", turns *altitude* into "attitude" and *aussi loin* into "aussie loins". Considering the literary meaning for loins—the region of the sexual organs regarded as the source of erotic or procreative power—we can read into this as saying that, besides the attitude (Mallarmé's hifalutin-ness), his literature (his sexual organ) hangs, much like the shape of the poetry on the page, a little to the right (regarding male genitalia) and it was only right (as in adroit, not politically to the right) once it had fused with the "errors and wrecks" caused by its intertextual relations.

Further down the page, zooming in on the lines: "veiled / doubting / roly-poly / brillianted emetic // I want to see Rita of the collapsible derrière oh sacred"; Rita, here, and her strangely attractive derrière (perhaps a half-pun on Derrida), in causing this shiny vomit of a poem to emit from Edwards, surely comes to represent the promiscuity of the pun and its ability to collapse the sign and the signified.

aussi

To end the poem, Edwards mistranslates *Toute Pensée émet Un Coup de dés* ("All Thought emits a Throw of the Dice") into "toupéed one my little mate I guess you'll want the code word eh?" Where Mallarmé rounds out his poem almost neatly with an openly enigmatic and existential poetic statement (on how each thought emits a ripple into the universe, affecting the course of history, perhaps), Edwards plays the parodist by presuming that the reader will want to find the code word in the final, epiphanic line of the poem, as if with a code word they might be able to solve the poem, as many have tried to with *Un Coup de dés*. It's a sly comment on how gnomic Mallarmé is (and how gnomic poetry can come to seem to readers who seek singular or straight meanings in language and, by extension, in their being in the world). Edwards' conclusion is also a bizarrely prescient comment on the future gnomic leader of the so-called free world, that "toupéed one" who may want the code word for nuclear weapons at some point. After all, Australia's "little mate", when it comes to political and military ties (and, dare I say, expediency), is always the President of the United States of America.

or

Fig. 12. Casper the Friendly Ghost (with cat), screenshot from *Casper the Friendly Ghost* (1945).

I thought to suggest that Chris Edwards is like Casper, the Friendly Ghost, with a gentle abjection borne out of Bataille. But, considering his view that writing poetry is "play *space*-time",[96] I'm beginning to think that Edwards' all-seeing Eye and disembodied voice are those of the Transformer, Unicron (quite literally a "Solar Anus")—a robot who

[96] Edwards, "Interview with Chris Edwards" (my emphasis).

can transform into a planet in the shape of a massive eye that can see into the Abyss of space, and who, with a quietly deep, futuristic voice, attracts space junk and other gutter-dwellers, other abysmal life (textually speaking) toward him—"a god of chaos who devours realities"[97] …

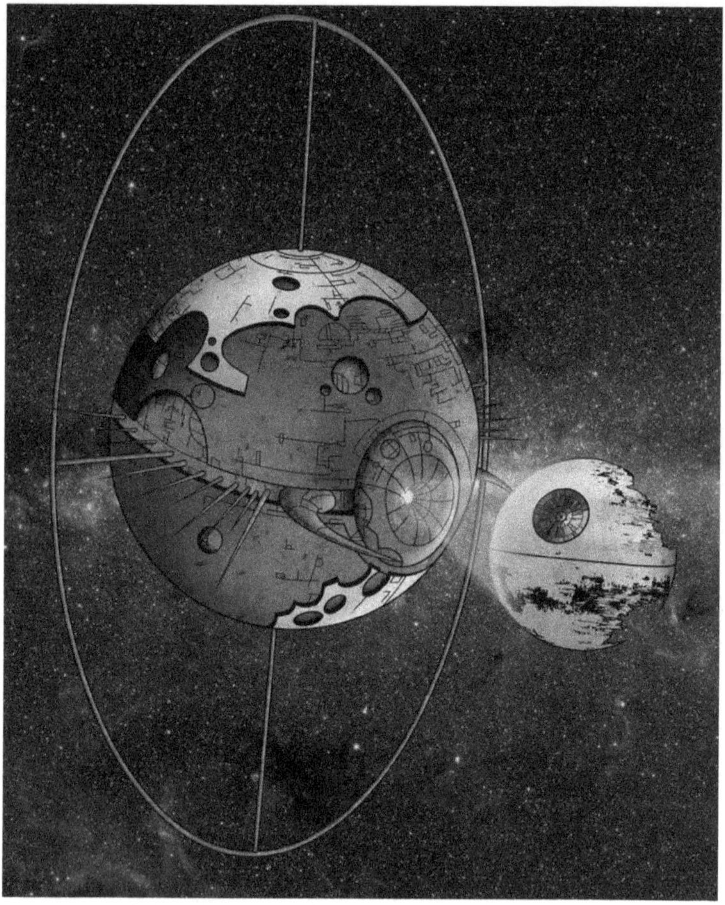

Fig. 13. Unicron eats the Death Star, *Deviant Art*, 2012.[98]

[97] "Unicron", *Wikipedia*, https://en.wikipedia.org/wiki/Unicron.

[98] See also: "Unicron transforming", *Youtube*, to hear his voice, see him transform and attract objects and others toward him: https://www.youtube.com/watch?v=TG4GaPcLgOs.

or

… is he a unicorn?

or

Perhaps Edwards is taking a leaf (toking a life / talking a loaf / teaking a loft) from (or with) James Joyce who, in his Cyclops episode of *Ulysses*, parodied, through plentiful and rude punning, the Apostles' Creed (the statement of Christian belief dating from the fourth century; ostensibly drafted by the twelve apostles of Jesus):

> They believe in rod, the scourger almighty, creator of hell upon earth and in Jacky Tar, the son of a gun, who was conceived of unholy boast, born of the fighting navy, suffered under rump and dozen, was scarified, flayed and curried, yelled like bloody hell, the third day he arose again from the bed, steered into haven, sitteth on his beamend till further orders whence he shall come to drudge for a living and be paid.[99]

aussi

etre un autre // Esprit // pour le jeter

as at the neither either // nor or // of the Spirit self-jettisoned

Edwards plays cleverly on a reader's proclivity to read sexual puns (like Joyce's "beamend" above) into the text. His deliberate paranomastic tactics of lapsus and misreading mean that even words he has not mistranslated can just as easily be misread by the reader. Take the above fragment. To have the vagueness of "the Spirit" (not to mention the *self*) jettisoned is often Edwards' prerogative in his poems, but his queer and deliberate *in*appropriation of the high-minded language of Mallarmé, his sexualising of its content, his use of litotes (to downplay his intentions but emphasise play with another)—allowed this reader to see "*Spirit* self-jettisoned" as "*Spirt* self-jettisoned".

[99] James Joyce, *Ulysses: The 1922 Text* (New York: University of Oxford Press, 2008), 315.

or

If there is a spirit in Edwards' "diversional dance" with Mallarmé, it's an impersonal, apparitional one, a colourful ghost in some choreography by Loïe Fuller—Fuller, whose ballet choreographies pre-figured modern dance, and perhaps even anticipated the imagery and movement of strange attractors through an art without definition and semiotic limitations.[100]

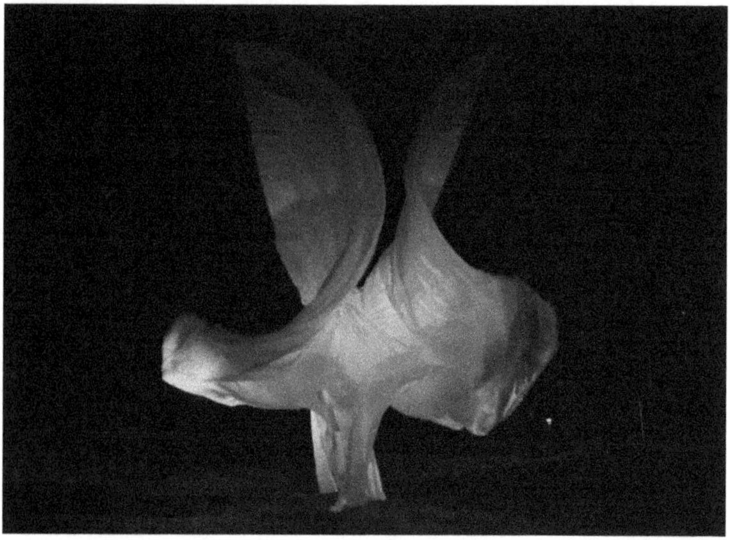

Fig. 14. A still from Loïe Fuller's *La danse des couleurs*, as conceived by Brygida Ochaim (1988).[101]

[100] Could Loïs Fuller, who invented new forms of dance in the last decade of the nineteenth century as *Un Coup de dés* was being composed, be described as the Mallarmé of dance, or should Mallarmé, who after all wrote of ballet and Fuller and how dance is like poetry, be described as the Loïs Fuller of poetry? For an essay on Mallarmé and Fuller, poetry and dance, see Susan Jones, "A Poetics of Potentiality: Mallarmé, Fuller, Yeats, and Graham", in *Literature, Modernism, and Dance* (Oxford: Oxford University Press, 2013), 13–43.

[101] Loïe Fuller and Brygida Ochaim, *La Danse des couleurs*, Bienale de la danse, 1988, https://numeridanse.com/en/publication/loie-fuller-la-danse-des-couleurs-3/.

aussi

Edwards' "dance of paragons"[102] is, to return to the perverse twenty-first century, both a symptom and a subversion of the post-digital age, in which fake news is real news, is cut-and-pasted, nay, mistranslated into your browser; an age in which wowsers and identity politics are at fever pitch; an age in which the problems of authorship and originality are arguably more global and intense than ever because the mediums and media in and through which we write, now becoming fully automated, often erroneously, have expanded so rapidly via an economic capitalisation of coding, hypertext, and computer-generated text; an age in which Generative Artificial Intelligence (GenAI) has become institutionalised not just into the corporate world replete with its marketing apparatuses, the political sphere and its public messaging, and the reproductive 24/7 news cycle, but also into the realm of education, making a mess and a mockery of the formative stages of any writer's and reader's (any student of the world's) agency and relation to language. The work, the writing and reading, of a mistranslation such as "A Fluke" is the antithesis of GenAI modes of writing and reading. The flattened-out language appropriations of GenAI, based on the mean expectations of millions of data inputs, resulting in clichés and parodies of the real, dampen the imagination while the appropriations of a mistranslation ensconce writer and reader in the morphing, licking flames of thought and association triggered by words. "A Fluke" is

fused with the wrecked and disorderly

whore of the internet's
quantified signal
engendering
saloon tales obliquities and declivities
on fire[103]

at the same time as attempting to "interrogate the real so dissolute". Mallarmé is "awkward in the original". His "doubts and nagging susurrations justify the crime" of Edwards' jokey "generated" "translation". All of Mallarmé's and Edwards' "parallelised neutralities identify as the

[102] Edwards, "A Fluke", 61.
[103] Edwards, "A Fluke", 61.

gaffe", or the "gap", between subject and object, sign and signified, sense and nonsense, truth and untruth, in a post-truth world.[104]

or

Perhaps the last word on Edwards' mistranslation is the first word, as in Edwards' epigraph, from Bataille's "Solar Anus": "It is clear that the world is purely parodic—in other words, that each thing seen is the parody of another, or is the same thing in a deceptive form".[105] Here the strange attractor of Mallarmé's proto-avant-guardist poem is queered in the abject flukes, fractal objects, and "bio-hazards"—"disruptive versions of human subjectivity that are dangerously prankish (*le blague*)"[106]—of Edwards' parody. No mere fluke, this anti-version unsettles its own multidimensional imaginary and ontological space—yes, "a like shipwreck", a "puerile shadow", and yet its own solar anus, its own black hole—on the bright *carte blanche* of the page.

[104] Edwards, "A Fluke", 56–61.

[105] Bataille epigraph, trans. Allan Stoekl, in Edwards, *A Fluke: A mistranslation of Stéphane Mallarmé's "Un Coup de dés..."*

[106] Fagan, "'A Fluke? [N]ever!'", 8.

5

John Tranter's "Desmond's Coupé" is a tract in the spirit of Brennan's "Musicopoematographoscope" (whose own anger he criticised, ironically) only the spirit is purple, far more Rimbaudian in Tranter's take-down of the comparably goody two-shoes Mallarmé. On the development of Tranter's poetics, Fagan and Peter Minter have argued that

> By 1968 Tranter was navigating a chiasmic cultural parallax, attracted to both American metropoetic and post-Romantic French Symbolism. This contest defines the direction of his first three books—the final "crisis" of which is played out in *The Alphabet Murders*. Tranter's solution to history was an inverted, Orientalising dialectic, and its synthesis was in the seminal figure of Arthur Rimbaud.[107]

aussi

This "chiasmic cultural parallax" can be traced through Australian poetry's development of Symbolism in the second half of the twentieth century, specifically in the differing interpretations of Rimbaud and Mallarmé by John Tranter and Robert Adamson (two of the central protagonists of the Generation of '68). In "Feral Symbolists: Robert Adamson, John Tranter and the Response to Rimbaud", David Brooks points out the irony of Tranter being more fond of Rimbaud despite his poetry becoming more Mallarméan but in a secular way, and of Adamson being more fond of Mallarmé despite his biographical affinities with Rimbaud.[108] He argues that in the 1970s Tranter emerges from his personal poetic crisis (no longer able to sustain the Rimbaudian *voyant* mode) into an anti-

[107] For a study of Tranter's dual modernist and postmodernist trajectory in Australian poetry since the 1960s, see Kate Fagan and Peter Minter, "Murdering Alphabets, Disorienting Romance: John Tranter and Postmodern Australian Poetics", *Jacket* 27 (April 2005): http://jacketmagazine.com/27/faga-mint.html.

[108] David Brooks, "Feral Symbolists: Robert Adamson, John Tranter, and the Response to Rimbaud", *Australian Literary Studies* 16.3 (1994): 280–8.

metaphysical mode after writing his poem "Rimbaud and the Pursuit of the Modern Heresy", whereas at the same time Adamson leans even more into metaphysical mode after writing a translation of Yves Bonnefoy's poem "Theatre". Both poems were published by Adamson, as editor of *New Poetry* (in 1974). Brooks suggests that Tranter's lines, "dead poet burning like a virus, / tainting the pages of a thousand magazines— / here is a thin talent shrieking imitation, there / an old man, uneasy with a maudlin respect", were aimed at Adamson, and that Adamson's "Theatre", in the way it doubles down on the "thaumaturgic", the metaphysical and the Muse, is a direct response to Tranter (Adamson was also attempting to amplify such Mallarméan concepts that he believed Bonnefoy had misconceived).[109]

In the years thereafter, the two precocious poets thinly critiqued each other in poems and interviews.[110] For one poetic example, when Adamson traduces Rimbaud's *Aprés le Dèluge* into "Rimbaud Having a Bath" (1981), he is battling the ghost of a Rimbaudian Tranter while overdetermining the translation to augment his concept of the Muse. Tranter's final word on the Rimbaud-Mallarmé-Tranter-Adamson schism occurs in his homophonic mistranslation of Mallarmé's *Un Coup de Dés*, "Desmond's Coupé" of 2006, which subsequently appeared in his collection *Starlight: 150 Poems* (2010).

Tranter's later works of poetry, *Starlight* and *Heart Starter* (2015), navigate the aforementioned chiasmic cultural parallax but with heightened parody. In these works he responds incessantly to canonised poems with constraint-based versions and anti-versions of his own—"an ambiguously postcolonial strategy"[111]—so as to simultaneously uphold and trouble European and American modern and postmodern poetic traditions. In *Starlight*, Tranter returns to Rimbaud and Mallarmé with a matured secular conceptualisation. *Starlight* contains computer-aided mistranslations and revisions of poems by *Symbolistes* Baudelaire, Verlaine, Rimbaud, and Mallarmé, as well as of works by seminal American poets also influenced

[109] David Brooks, "Feral Symbolists", 283–4.

[110] For one telling interview, see, for instance, Robert Adamson, "The Truth I Know: An Interview with Robert Adamson by John Tranter", *Makar* 14.1 (1978): 3–13.

[111] David McCooey, "Review Short: John Tranter's *Heart Starter*", *Cordite Poetry Review*, August 25, 2015, http://cordite.org.au/reviews/mccooey-tranter/.

by the French, T.S. Eliot and John Ashbery. In the spirit of Brennan's "Musicopoematographoscope" and Rimbaud's *Album Zutique* (1880s, later published in 1943, a collection of abject pastiche of the Parnassian style as parodied by Rimbaud and some thirteen others), "Desmond's Coupé" is a self-reflexive and abject tirade toward the poetic urge to highfalutin-ness, and by extension a swipe at Adamson's Mallarmé-worshipping: "Desmond's coupé is full of jam. / He's in a quandary: a bean lance, or a dance of circumstances. / He's eternally fond of his own naivety".[112] Desmond, as a play on *dés* (dice) and *monde* (world) while sharing letters and sounds with "Adamson", could well be representing the poetic worlds of both Mallarmé and Adamson (as a Mallarmé wannabe).

or

More specifically, Tranter's inversion of *Un Coup de dés* is an uncomplicatedly left-justified, jokey dream narrative that undercuts Mallarmé's inability to make a narrative decision. Its punctuated Ashberyesque or Surrealist flow of ideas, speechiness and sound-association allows for the geriatric Desmond to stumble about and actually encounter other life forms (unlike the Master in *Un Coup de dés*), and for the speaker(s) of the poem to undermine the conceits of Mallarmé's notion of the "pure work" (*oeuvre pure*). Despite its distance in form and syntax from Edwards' version, the poem's generative technique was the same for Tranter: it's largely a homophonic mistranslation that toys with transformational, paranomastic techniques.

If we look for the full mistranslation of Mallarmé's title *UN COUP DE DÉS JAMAIS N'ABOLIRA LE HASARD*, embedded in the free verse stanzas of Tranter's poem, we get (in non-capitals): "Desmond's coupé is full of jam but that won't abolish folly in Hansard",[113] which seems a deliberate nod to Edwards' "noble lie", and to any truth that an authority, political or otherwise, might pretend to wield—Hansard being the name for the verbatim transcripts of Parliamentary Debates in most Commonwealth countries.[114]

112 John Tranter, *Starlight: 150 Poems* (St. Lucia: University of Queensland Press, 2010), 15.

113 Tranter, *Starlight*, 15–21.

114 The word Hansard also arguably dates back to the records of the Hanseatic League, for Baltic trade.

aussi

The poem becomes a "disrespectful pie", as Tranter states in his University of Wollongong doctoral thesis, "in the face" of not only Mallarmé (and Adamson), but of literary decorum and tradition.[115] Writing in the third person, ironically, and possibly as a parody of the split subject, he quotes himself describing his own mistranslation of *Un Coup de dés*:

> dealing with the work of an important poet like Mallarmé takes us into the realm of the "anxiety of influence", as Harold Bloom labelled it: the need to learn from past masters without being overwhelmed by their mastery, and the need for any artist to clear the undergrowth of history to make room for her or his own new work. That uneasy mixture of respect and aggression colours my poem.[116]

But does Tranter suppose that his methods for dealing with his influences are entirely conscious and intentional? If so, he perhaps misunderstands Bloom, who insists on the salience of misrecognition: in one of his seven ratios of misreading, Bloom explains that any writer taking on the burden of tradition enacts an unconscious "swerving" or "misprision", so as to make it new and avoid the accumulating anxiety of past excellence. The "swerving" is the law of the clinamen here, again, but take "misprision" too, which Bloom adopts/adapts from Shakespeare's "Sonnet 87", an erotic poem that he rather reads as an allegory of any writer's relation to tradition: "'Misprision' for Shakespeare, as opposed to 'mistaking', implied not only a misunderstanding or misreading but tended also to be a punning word-play suggesting unjust imprisonment."[117]

[115] Tranter's doctoral thesis, "Distant Voices", contains a creative component called *Vocoder*—a collection of poems that make up the first three-quarters of his subsequently published collection *Starlight*—plus an exegetical component in which Tranter provides notes to all the poems in *Vocoder*, historical notes to all his published books of poetry, and an essay about dream-work and how his three main influences (Rimbaud, John Ashbery and the hoax poet Ern Malley) have come to bear on his poetics. The exegesis is a fascinating self-portrait and would be worth studying purely for the psychoanalytical aspects of how an author sees, or cannot see, certain aspects of their own work.

[116] Tranter, "Distant Voices", 118.

[117] Harold Bloom, preface to *The Anxiety of Influence: A Theory of Poetry*, Second Edition (New York: Oxford University Press, 1997), xiii.

or

Is Tranter trapped?

or

While Bloom overlooks (and elsewhere downplays) the erotic and its role in the *affairs* of influence (see my previous analysis on the "promiscuity of the pun" in Edwards for one such affair), perhaps he has unconsciously lifted the idea of the linguistic swerve from a forebear of his own. In *The Burden of the Past on the English Poet*, W. Jackson Bate opens by quoting Samuel Johnson on the topic: "It is, indeed, always *dangerous* to be placed in a state of unavoidable comparison with excellence", and then unpacks the "original, rather ominous sense" of the word "dangerous": "it means 'having lost one's freedom', having become 'dominated' … subjected to the tyranny of something outside one's own control … A cognate is our word 'dungeon'".[118] There's no mention of Bate's danger or dungeon in Bloom, but if he has read Bate, he couldn't possibly have misread him—surely not—taking on some of his ideas and swerving unconsciously from them … No, no room for misprision in Bloom …

aussi

Back to the prison/prism of "Desmond's Coupé". Tranter's constant re-negotiation of his literary forebears, his choice to revel/rebel in versions and anti-versions, could be read as his conscious act to avoid said danger. But how language filters through him—as in, playing with poetic techniques that "cede the initiative to words", perhaps prismatically—is a process that relies on, or is indivisible from, the unconscious. No matter how much he signposts his intentions with copious notes and witty asides as to his procedures (see his doctoral thesis), the symbolic Other of language is beyond his control.[119] It's almost as if Tranter over-

[118] W. Jackson Bate, *The Burden of the Past and the English Poet* (London: Chatto & Windus, 1971), 3.

[119] Jacques Lacan repeatedly refers to "the unconscious" as "the discourse of the Other", where the Other is the symbolic structure of language. See Lacan, "Seminar on 'The Purloined Letter'", *Yale French Studies* 0.48 (1972): 45, http://xroads.virginia.edu/~DRBR2/lacan2.pdf.

explains his homosocial dalliance with his male poetic forebears to hide the anxiety of misprision taking place (Thou doth protest too much.). In any event, "Desmond's Coupé", as artefact of the poetic process, and as abject experiment, certainly comes out swerving. Mallarmé's *sauf … que le rencontre ou l'effleure une toque de minuit / et immobillise,*[120] for instance, becomes in Tranter's misprision (or Desmond's dungeon): "so far, so good, // where recounting the effluent is the talk of the minute / and it immobilises you".[121]

or

While offering a self-consciously aggressive critique of Mallarméan poetics, "Desmond's Coupé" is also extremely funny and jazzy. Punning on the French *du gouffre*, Tranter resurrects the clarinet player Jimmy Giuffre and then, in true ventriloquist mode, has him playing guitar, as though he's a member of Tranter's own covers band. Mallarmé might be a master of the enigma, but Tranter is a master of prosopopoeia, which is the speech of an imaginary person, or the conjuring of an imaginary other to speak to or through, or, it is the personification of an abstract thing (that thing being, in the above instance, one of Mallarmé's words). Dozens of Aussie characters flit through Tranter's tract, each allowing him to banter with the dead Mallarmé (and Adamson). On top of homophonic mistranslation, Tranter improvises a number of times with flourishes of word-sound association.

This is how and where Tranter appears and reappears like Disney's Cheshire Cat, distortedly reiterating and purposefully overdetermining Mallarmé's fragments of *pure literature*. From the French, *avance retombée d'un mal* à *dresser le vol / et couvrant les jaillissements / coupant au ras les bonds*, Tranter has, "makes him think he's dead and buried or makes him realise he's a bad dresser on a plane or in jail / but you don't dress for jail / and people don't wear a jacket on a plane anymore. / Raise the bonds" (a description of the once-jailed Adamson?). Later, Tranter manipulates the French, *le temps / de souffleter / bifurcées // un roc*, into "Time to snaffle / a bifurcated soufflé, / thinks the old bird."[122] "Desmond's Coupé" is rife

[120] Mallarmé, *Collected Poems*, 136–7.
[121] Tranter, *Starlight*, 18.
[122] Tranter, *Starlight*, 15–8.

with these mini car crashes of sound and sally. And, at times, Tranter comes across like Australia's John Ashbery, in terms of being a medium for the vernacular, of pursuing dream-like narratives and representing the movement of thought, only Tranter also has ulterior motives and a more parodic bent, as well as a more scathing and cynical tone, "where recounting the effluent is the talk of the minute".[123]

Fig. 15. Cheshire Cat, screenshot from *Alice in Wonderland* (1951).

Tranter's inversion of *Un Coup de dés* is designed as pure entertainment, taking pleasure at the expense of Mallarmé while firing off a veiled final shot across the bows at his Down Under poetic adversary in Adamson. His gambit is replete with downplaying Aussie vernacular, abjectivity, and naughty banter—its goofy narrative simultaneously spoofs Mallarmé's notion of the "pure work" (*oeuvre pure*) (and Adamson's appropriation of it), or, as Edwards' version would say, "gives it the finger".[124]

[123] Tranter, *Starlight*, 11.
[124] Edwards, "A Fluke", 51.

6

Throughout "A Fluke" and "Desmond's Coupé" there are dozens of mistranslated suitors that resonate for Edwards and Tranter: in both, *ombre* becomes "hombre"; *enfouie* becomes "phooey"; *sombre* becomes "sombrero"; and *barbe soumise* becomes "barbequed sunset" in Edwards and "barbeque or so you surmise" in Tranter.

Interestingly, "*CE SERAIT*" ("it would be") is translated by both Edwards and Tranter into pseudo-Spanish: "*QUE SERA*" for Edwards, and "*que sera, sera*" by Tranter. *Que sera sera* ("What will be, will be") is an exclamation used to convey a cheerful fatalistic recognition that future events may be out of the speaker's control. (Could *Un Coup de dés* be a long drawn-out analogy for this sentiment?) The phrase rose to popularity as the title of a pop song from 1955, written by Jay Livingston and Ray Evans and introduced by Doris Day in Alfred Hitchcock's film *The Man Who Knew Too Much* (1956) as a cue to her onscreen kidnapped son. Do Tranter and Edwards know too much, or did Mallarmé? Is Mallarmé the kidnapped son of Tranter and Edwards?

aussi

Reading these four poems side by side—*Un Coup de dés* and its "veiled inversions at a juncture whose supremacy's probably // celluloid / oh puerile shadow" (as "A Fluke" describes them)[125]—at some point they begin to merge into each other's shadows and superimpose. In the line: "… *and gives it the finger // COMME ÇA*",[126] Edwards can be seen as translating Tranter. In the lines: "eating soup and getting vaguer / … he enters the aisle, bending his knee / like a bat flopping into the sea,"[127] Tranter could be transmuting Brennan. In the lines: "the fair white page

[125] Edwards, "A Fluke", 48.
[126] Edwards, "A Fluke", 51.
[127] Tranter, *Starlight*, 17.

// whose candour / illumes / the mystic signs /// Abracadabra,"[128] Brennan might be commenting on Edwards. And, strangely enough, Mallarmé comes to translate all his Australian mistranslators in the lines:

AS IF
An insinuation simple
in the silence enrolled with irony
or
the mystery
hurled
howled

in some nearby whirlpool of hilarity and horror",[129]

i.e. in Australia.

or

Who is haunting whom, here?

aussi

During the first drafts of this essay, a plagiarism scandal in Australian poetry was creating a whirlpool of hilarity and horror in which Sigmund Freud was invoked: "Everywhere the signs that a poet has been here before me".[130] One poet in particular was accused of not citing his theft of other writers' lines, lines that included this Freud doozy. The poet's defense was that they were writing centos. In terms of any potential charges of plagiarism,[131] Brennan's, Edwards' and Tranter's mistranslations recall pre-eighteenth-

[128] Brennan, "Musicopoematographoscope", 17.

[129] Mallarmé, *Collected Poems*, 134–5.

[130] For a brief summary of this plagiarism scandal, see Toby Fitch, "Plagiarism scandal has revealed an ugly side of Australian poetry", *The Guardian*, September 23, 2013, http://www.theguardian.com/commentisfree/2013/sep/23/australian-poetry-plagiarism.

[131] The term plagiarism comes from the Latin *plagiarius*, which literally means "kidnapper", and dates back to the first century AD, according to the *Oxford English Dictionary*. The history of plagiarism is a long and complicated one and I don't intend to rewrite it. In the end, this study of mistranslation is conducted in the spirit of epistemological anarchism: not seeking to find the solution to issues such as plagiarism, but rather

century attitudes toward originality, or what was called "creative imitation", whereby the imitation and strategic revision of prior authors was a kind of "filial rejection with respect". Moreover/move over, as Northrop Frye jokes in *Anatomy of Criticism*: "any serious study of literature soon shows that the real difference between the original and the imitative poet is simply that the former is more profoundly imitative".[132] *Serio Ludere* again.

or

The imitative elements of a homophonic translation and creative imitation seem to allow, or even encourage, a kind of jokey vitriol, an ironic deadpanning in the translator. I tend to think of Brennan's, Edwards' and Tranter's inversions as three big jokes. They certainly adhere to Freud's theories on jokes. He wrote of how jokes are an interaction between unconscious drives and conscious thoughts, and he believed that jokes let out forbidden thoughts and feelings that the conscious mind usually suppresses in deference to society.[133]

aussi

Anne Carson psychoanalyses a crisis in Hölderlin's translations, which were idiosyncratic, went through years of compulsive revision, "forcing the text from strange to more strange", and used increasingly violent choices for words as he closed in on his own madness:

playfully misreading those issues so as to uncover various absurdities that might generate new critical excursions through aesthetics.

132 Northrop Frye et al., "Imitation", in *The Princeton Encyclopedia of Poetry and Poetics: Fourth Edition*, eds. Greene et al. (Princeton: Princeton University Press, 2012), 675–7.

133 Each of the mistranslations analysed in this essay could fit, at various instances, all three of Freud's categories for jokes: 1) The mimetic joke: which is a process involving two different representations of the body in our mind. For example, in the phrase "Their hearts are in the right place," the heart has two representations. One is anatomical while the other is metaphorical; 2) Tendentious jokes: which are jokes that have to contain lust, hostility or both; and 3) Non-tendentious jokes, where the joke applies "to one and the same act of ideation, two different ideational methods". See Sigmund Freud, *Jokes and Their Relation to the Unconscious*, Vol. 6 of the Pelican Freud Library, 1905, trans. James Strachey (New York: W. W. Norton, 1960), 132–67.

> Maybe Hölderlin was pretending to be mad the whole time, I don't know. What fascinates me is to see his catastrophe, at whatever consciousness he chose it, as a method extracted from translation, a method organised by the rage against cliché. After all what else is one's own language but a gigantic cacophonous cliché. Nothing has not been said before. The templates are set. Adam long ago named all the creatures. Reality is captured.[134]

When one approaches the blank white page (as Mallarmé did so consciously), its empty surface is already filled with the whole history of writing up to that moment: "it is a compaction of all the clichés of representation" already extant in the writer's world, in a writer's head, in the probabilities of what can be done on this surface.[135]

The act of mistranslating, then—of writing over, through, or under a given text—is also a catastrophising, a method for disrupting or undercutting the originality of the original, but also a way of pointing to the inherent cliché in one's own language (the big joke of one's own language), and in poems of the canon, even knowingly mimetic, or repeatedly tampered with templates such as *Un Coup de dés*.

or

The word cliché was supposed to mimic the sound of the printer's die striking the metal, and is thus onomatopoeic, and a neologism for an untranslatable sound. In a sense, from its journey from action to word, you could call it a homophonic translation, or a mistranslation.[136]

[134] Anne Carson, *Nay Rather*, The Cahiers Series #21 (London: Sylph Editions, 2013), 18–20.

[135] This paragraph was paraphrased, switching "the painter" to "the writer", from Carson, *Nay Rather*, 20.

[136] According to Carson (*Nay Rather*, 4), "Cliché is a French borrowing, past participle of the verb *clicher*, a term from printing meaning 'to make a stereotype from a relief printing surface'. It has been assumed into English unchanged, partly because using French words makes English-speakers feel more intelligent and partly because the word has imitative origins (it is supposed to mimic the sound of the printer's die striking the metal) that make it untranslatable".

aussi

Both Mallarmé's and Derrida's writings are particularly self-conscious of mimesis. Mallarmé's prose poem "Mimique", beginning with the word "silence" and ending with "reading", plays on the varying meanings of mime and mimesis so as to demonstrate the inherent repetition and mimicry in writing, thus offering us a way to read his own work. Roger Pearson's description of the poem makes this clear: it's "a written text describing a silent mime, a mime (as event) by a mime (Margueritte) who has written a visible (but to the reader of 'Mimique' invisible) text … about a performance which is an unwritten page of monologue, itself a silent monologue in a dialogue with a soul (a reader of a dead wife) who doesn't speak."[137] And if we substitute "poet" or "poem" for "mime" in the previous description, we conjure a definition of Mallarmé as translator of silence.

or

"Mimique" is another example of Mallarmé's "*or*-play". It even contains the word *or* ("gold"), along with other classic Mallarméan words that create chains of association such as *fantôme* ("phantom", "shade", "shape"), *blanc* ("white", "blank", "space"), *hymen* (both "membrane" and, archaically, "marriage"), all of which, along with the poem's syntactical ambiguities, act out an imitation, not of a referent or a reality, but of the notion of mimesis itself:

> here anticipating, there recalling, in the future, in the past, *under the false appearance of a present.* That is how the Mime operates, whose act is confined to a perpetual allusion without breaking the ice or the mirror: he thus sets up a medium, a pure medium, of fiction … Surprise, accompanying the artifice of a notation of sentiments by unproffered sentences …
>
> *ici devançant, là remémorant, au futur, au passé,* sous une apparence fausse de présent. *Tel opère le Mime, dont le jeu se borne à une allusion perpétuelle sans briser la glace: il installe, ainsi, un milieu, pur, de fiction*

[137] Roger Pearson, *Mallarmé and Circumstance: The Translation of Silence* (Oxford: Clarendon, 2004), 65–6.

> … *Surprise, accompagnant l'artifice d'une notation de sentiments par phrases point proférées …*[138]

aussi

In "The Double Session, or Mallarmé's Miming of Mimesis" (*La double séance*), Derrida "executes a kind of '*pas de deux*'—both a dance of duplicity and an erasure of binality—with the history of a certain interpretation of *mimesis*".[139] What is initially striking about "The Double Session" is the suggestive typographic spacing. Derrida inserts Mallarmé's prose poem "Mimique" into an L-shaped quotation from Plato's *Philebus* (which is concerned with the nature of thinking and art); it has quotations in boxes from *Un Coup de dés* and *Le Livre*, too; it reproduces Mallarmé's handwriting at one point; and the pages are often loaded with footnotes. The reader's attention is clearly being directed to the syntactical function of spacing in the act of reading. Barbara Johnson, Derrida's translator, writes:

> Through such supplementary syntactical effects, Derrida duplicates and analyses the ways in which Mallarmé's texts mime their own articulation, include their own blank spaces among their referents, and deploy themselves consistently with one textual fold too many or too few to be accounted for by a reading that would seek only the text's "message" or "meaning". By thus making explicit the role of the materiality of space within the act of understanding, Mallarmé—and Derrida—demonstrate the untenability of the logocentric distinction between the sensible and the intelligible, between ideality and materiality.[140]

Derrida argues that mime—and by implication, writing—doesn't imitate or copy some prior phenomena, idea, or figure, but constitutes the phantasm of the original in and through the mime:

> He represents nothing, imitates nothing, does not have to conform to any prior referent with the aim of achieving adequation or verisimilitude … We are faced then with mimicry imitating nothing:

[138] Mallarmé, "Mimique", in Derrida, "Translator's Introduction", in *Dissemination*, 1972, trans. Barbara Johnson (Chicago: University of Chicago Press, 1981), xx–xxii and 175.

[139] Barbara Johnson, in Derrida "Translator's Introduction", in *Dissemination*, xxvii.

[140] Johnson, "Translator's Introduction", xxviii–xxix.

> faced, so to speak, with the double … that nothing anticipates, nothing at least, that is not itself already double. There is no simple reference ... this speculum reflects no reality: it produces mere "reality-effects" ... in this speculum with no reality, in this mirror of a mirror, a difference or dyad does exist, since there are mimes and phantoms. But it is a difference without reference, or rather reference without a referent, without any first or last unit, a ghost that is the phantom of no flesh.[141]

or

The ante-simulacrum, the pre-copy of a copy.

aussi

Throughout "The Double Session" Derrida puns on Plato's *antre* ("cave") and Mallarmé's *entre* ("between"). What he's getting at is a characterisation of the "space of writing"—in which writing is not the revelation of truth but an "event" ("hymen, crime, suicide, spasm") where "the simulacrum is a [perpetual] transgression", and where—to continue the sexual metaphor—binaries such as desire and presence, void and fulfillment, become indistinguishable, collapsed, folded over/into one another. The page, the folded tissue or veil of the hymen, is transgressed, but it's "fiction": "What takes place is only the *entre* (between), the place, the spacing, which is nothing …" Endless mirrors, a deadlock of meaning, where "nothing happens", becoming suspense: "Hymen in perpetual motion: one can't get out of Mallarmé's *antre* as one can out of Plato's cave. Never min(e)d [*mine de rien*]".[142]

or

Maybe all this caving, this gutter spelunking, is a kind of "ontospeleology", a term derived from the Greek words for "being" and "cave", and which Derrida

[141] Derrida, "The Double Session", in *Dissemination*, 206.

[142] In French, *mine de rien* means, in its colloquial sense, "as though it were of no importance"; but literally it can mean "a mine full of nothing" (in Derrida, "The Double Session", 208–16).

has described as "another name for mimetology".[143] Or perhaps it's just the return of the concept of eternal return, applied to the problem of representation.

or

In returning to Derrida's suggestive typography, where "Mimique" is inserted into Plato's cave full of shadows, and where a play of representation seems endless, one doesn't have to think of this concept in Nietzschean terms, as if "some day or night a demon [might] steal after you into your loneliest loneliness and say to you: 'This life as you now live it and have lived it, you will have to live once more and innumerable times more …'"[144] The inability of a text, of literature, of genre, to escape its own terms, and to escape the play of representation, doesn't have to be interpreted as such a limitation. Mallarmé proves this. And so does Edwards, especially. For instance, is not the gutter to Mallarmé what the cave is to Plato, just in a new configuration? And is not the gutter to Edwards—in which the gutter exists literally in the work but also figuratively between his work and Mallarmé's—a cave within a cave, a cave outside a cave, and a cave between a cave, in which a new dimension is breached?

or

Existing *entre* the *antre*, Mallarmé's *Un Coup de dés* tears the page, while, *entre* the *autre antre*, Edwards' "A Fluke" tears the shadow of the page. Edwards' homo-erotic imagery and metaphors in his doubling over of Mallarmé's text make "A Fluke" a literal inversion, meanwhile tearing heterosexual or cis-literature a new one, so to speak.

aussi

Derrida's writings are useful in explaining how a text, how literature, is always multiple, doubled. In his essays, but particularly in "The Law of Genre" (*genre* in French also means "gender"), Derrida shows how

143 In his notebook for "Comment C'est", Samuel Beckett uses the term "ontospeleology" to describe the subject of his writings. See Samuel Beckett, *Comment C'est How It Is And / et L'image: A Critical-Genetic Edition*, ed. Edouard Magessa O'Reilly (New York and London: Routledge, 2001). See also Derrida, *Dissemination*, 40.

144 Friedrich Nietzsche, *The Gay Science*, 1887, trans. Walter Kaufmann (New York: Vintage, 1974), 341.

language is always structured from its opposite, its other. Through two important rhetorical tropes, *chiasmas* (repeated inversion/reversal of words) and *catachresis* (taking a metaphor to extremes), he explores the relationship between *citation* and *récit* (re-citation)—or language versus speech—and how such binaries, when examined extensively, cannot hold up over multiple iterations. He makes the argument that any category that arises (say, a poem, or a visual poem) seems to come from within itself, but also from outside. It comes from both outside and inside, hence Derrida's imagistic use of invagination and (en)folding.[145]

or

The Klein bottle is an example of a non-orientable surface; it's a two-dimensional manifold against which a system for determining a normal vector cannot be consistently defined. It's a one-sided surface which, if travelled upon, could be followed back to the point of origin while flipping the traveller upside down. Another related non-orientable object is the Möbius strip. Whereas a Möbius strip is a surface with boundary, a Klein bottle has no boundary (conversely, a sphere is an orientable surface with no boundary).[146]

[145] Derrida, "The Law of Genre", trans. Avital Ronell, *Glyph: Textual Studies* 7 (1980): 202–32.

[146] The Klein bottle was first described in 1882 by German mathematician Felix Klein. Incidentally, it may have originally been named the Kleinsche Fläche ("Klein surface") but was then misinterpreted as Kleinsche Flasche ("Klein bottle"), which ultimately led to the adoption of its current term. See Francis Bonahon, *Low-Dimensional Geometry: from Euclidean Surfaces to Hyperbolic Knots* (Providence: American Mathematical Society, 2009), 95. For active gif, see: https://plus.maths.org/content/os/issue26/features/mathart/kleinBottle_anim.

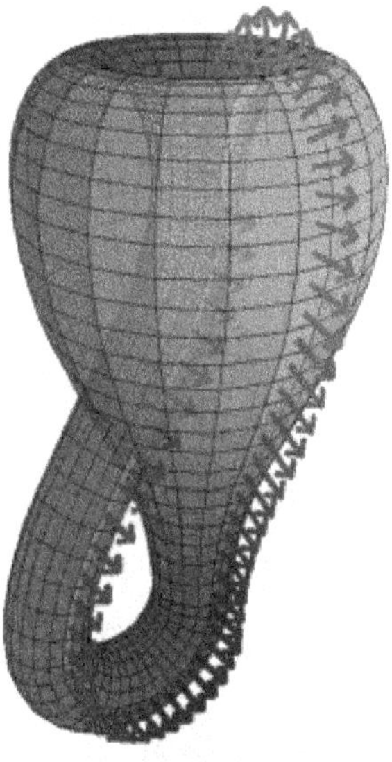

Fig. 16. Konrad Polthier, Klein Bottle, *Plus Magazine* (2003).

aussi

In *Of Grammatology* (his science of writing) Derrida inverts the assumption that writing represents speech. He explains that, in the "play of representation", we don't know which is the chicken and which the egg, because if writing is the representor—the mirror—it thereby reflects speech and things, distorting and perverting them. It splits what it represents and offers up a trace, a *différance*, a double, a supplement, a spectre (all key Derridean terms). Writing is

> A dangerous promiscuity and a nefarious complicity between the reflection and the reflected which lets itself be seduced narcissistically. In this play of representation, the point of origin becomes ungraspable. There are things like reflecting pools, and images, an infinite reference from one to the other, but no longer a source, a spring. There is no longer a simple origin. For what is reflected is split *in itself* and not only as an addition to itself of its image. The reflection, the image, the double, splits what it doubles. The origin

of the speculation becomes a difference. What can look at itself is not one; and the law of the addition of the origin to its representation, of the thing to its image, is that one plus one makes at least three.[147]

or

Fig. 17. Timescape of Chopin's *Mazurka Op. 68 No. 3, CHARM: AHRC* (2009).[148]

In other words, we can't escape on any level how writing is a play of representation, how writing is always already illicit play, our "nefarious complicity" with "meaning". What we think are truths are "in fact" already multi-face(te)d. Our attempts at "meaning" are reductive. What we try to reduce to a singularity is already three-dimensional. Truth in writing is a chimera, yet traces of truth are there—via the "living presence" of

[147] Derrida, *Of Grammatology*, 1967, trans. Gayatri Chakravorty Spivak (Baltimore: Johns Hopkins University Press, 1997), 36–7.

[148] This colorful triangle might look like abstract art, but it's actually a visual representation of the similarities between different recordings of the same piece of music. It's a "timescape". The horizontal axis represents time, and the colours show how similar the recording being analysed is to other specific recordings. What is being measured is the relative duration of each note, or the artist's unique rubato. The image is a timescape for Arthur Rubinstein's 1939 recording Chopin's *Mazurka Op. 68 No. 3*. See: *CHARM: AHRC Research Centre for the History and Analysis of Recorded Music*, http://www.charm.rhul.ac.uk/projects/p2_3_2.html.

speech, as Derrida calls it, through which "the signifier and the signified seem to unite".[149] Like the television, or film, or the phone, writing is a technology that reproduces ghosts. Truth is unreproducible > Writing is forever not > Righting feverish naughts > Writhing in forgery knots. Yet in the speech-y nonsense of punning, snippets of truth form.

aussi

According to Gelett Burgess, "Nonsense is the fourth dimension of literature".[150] This nonsense-mining fourth dimension is where the plays on words of Edwards' "A Fluke" and Tranter's "Desmond's Coupé" begin. Their poems offer "Surprise, accompanying the artifice of a notation" (from "Mimique", above). They foreground mimesis: we already know when we start to read that the phantasm of the original, the ante-simulacrum, is Mallarmé's *Un Coup de dés*. Homophonic translation is like a feedback loop gone loopy, glitchy. The foregrounding of mirrors and reflecting pools of representation reflect back distorted or disturbed magnifications—which whirl/whorl us into a fifth dimension, where representation equals re*prescient*ation—more *multi-nefarious* than before—and where "truth" and "meaning" become even more material, become "literal" again, not only space junk but the filaments in space too, whether we choose to see them or not. Some might need a Hubble telescope. It's the inverse of Mallarmé's white page. Edwards' and Tranter's inversions agitate and blink in black pools of the sky's cave(s).

or

According to Edwards, quoting Robert Duncan, a significant forebear of his:

> The poem … is "multiphasic", "polyvalent", space enmeshed in time, duration embedded in place (whether page or auditorium). As its recipients, we experience "the concords and contrasts in chronological sequence, as in a jigsaw puzzle [sic]," but Duncan also asks his readers (and listeners, presumably) to bear in mind "the time

[149] Derrida, *Positions*, 1972, trans. Alan Bass (Chicago: University of Chicago Press, 1981), 22.
[150] Gelett Burgess, *The Burgess Nonsense Book* (New York: Frederick A. Stokes Company, 1901).

> of the whole," in which "each part . . . is conceived as a member of every other part, having, as in a mobile, an interchange of roles".[151]

From there/here—with the poem vibrating above the Abyss as mobile, as constellation—it's up to us where we take our "play space-time", our imaginations. As Mallarmé puts it, "it is up to the poet, roused by a dare, to translate!"[152]

or

Do we need a new definition for translation? Attempting to offer a global classification of translation's linguistic aspects, Roman Jakobson distinguished three kinds:

1. intralingual translation, or paraphrase;
2. interlingual translation, or translation in the most common sense;
3. intersemiotic translation, in which, for example, verbal signs are reencoded in nonverbal sign systems.[153]

Yet each of these classifications presumes the existence of one initial language and one translation in the literal sense into another language, that is, that one language can be seamlessly transferred into another—that, as Derrida puts it, "each linguistic system has integrity".[154]

aussi

If we're going to categorise translation, then, we might also turn to Australian poet and critic Peter Porter for how, perhaps, not to cordon things off. In his essay (and book) on translation, "Saving from the Wreck"—a title that one could be mistaken for thinking might address the seaworthiness of translating a poem like *Un Coup de dés*—he rather plays the schoolteacher, helpfully laying out seven categories for how translation is done:

[151] Edwards, "Interview with Chris Edwards".
[152] Mallarmé, "Mimique", in Derrida, *Dissemination*, 175.
[153] Patrick Mahony, "Roundtable on Translation", in Derrida, *The Ear of the Other*, 1982, trans. Christie McDonald (Lincoln: University of Nebraska Press, 1988), 94–5.
[154] Derrida, "Roundtable on Translation", 100.

1. *Uncompromising Scholarly*;
2. *Aesthetic Scholarly*;
3. *Recreative Scholarly*;
4. *Exuberant Scholarly or Over the Top!*;
5. *Literal*;
6. *Imitation*; and,
7. *Ecumenical Slovenly*.[155]

Of almost all these categories Porter is scathing, in terms of what makes for a "successful" translation and not a shipwreck, exclaiming: "I think we simply have to admit that much of what passes for translation today is just organised dissemination of misinformation."[156] While Porter acknowledges overlaps in the types, he only mentions homophonic translation once: "More bewildering is Louis Zukofsky's aim in translating Catullus of finding English words which are homophones—or nearly so—while still being approximate translations of the Latin", and lumps this mode into *Uncompromising Scholarly*.[157] Of course, it wasn't simply Louis Zukofsky's work, but his wife Celia's too. Porter seems to overlook this gendered fact in much the same way he ignores other genres of translation, while narrowing the parameters of translation to what is sometimes and elsewhere referred to, in terms of a seamless semantic translation, as "transparent literalism".

Maria Tymoczko writes of the prevalence of this kind of translation, historically: "The history of Western European translation privileges an implicit literalism that has been used to disseminate the empires of religion, secular rule, and commerce throughout the last five hundred years."[158]

Despite Porter's conservative critique, which upholds the canon rather than recognising alternatives that twentieth and twenty-first century poetics have developed, he manages to concoct (within his categories) a couple of excellent descriptions that could also be applied to a category that I've been calling, up until now, "mistranslation", of which homophonic translation would be one fraction. On damning the process

[155] Peter Porter, "Saving from the Wreck", in *Saving from the Wreck* (Nottingham: Trent, 2001), 37–47.
[156] Porter, "Saving from the Wreck", 47.
[157] Porter, "Saving from the Wreck", 41.
[158] Maria Tymoczko, *Enlarging Translation, Empowering Translators* (Manchester: St. Jerome, 2007), 8.

of "Imitation" (another fraction of mistranslation)—of writing versions like those of Robert Lowell, for instance—he writes: "The basic rule seems to be that the translator finds in a finished work of art the bones of one of his own. He is struck by a form of pre-echo".[159]

or

What if the aim of a translation *is* the "dissemination of misinformation"? What if the aim was to illuminate—or even set fire to—pre-echoes? Homophonic translation is, after all, part-rendering and part-rubbishing of a forebear's work and, as demonstrated above, sometimes even becomes the pre-echo of the original, because writing always already peddles in the symbolic Other that is language (as per Lacan). Results have had to pass through the unconscious. Writing is always already a "translation"—of thought, or of internal monologue. A *mis*translation, through its wordplay techniques, its foregrounding of *latent* forms of language such as the pun, brings some of the unconscious elements to the surface, makes them "present", an event. Let's not forget, here, Mallarmé's *fil conducteur* and Edwards' "the latent conductor unreasoning verisimilitude imposes on the text". We could add to this Walter Redfern's "Puns are a latent resource of language". Disseminated throughout a poem, puns are "unearthed" by the poet during the ludic process of writing and only heightened in a mistranslation; puns "illuminate the nature of language" and make the reader a participant in the unearthing—an event that encourages collaboration.[160] On quoting Roland Barthes and his pleasure over puns, Redfern, ever the archivist, writes:

> Experimental psychologists have shown quantifiably what most people know instinctively and by experience: that it is authoritarian personalities who most dislike ambiguity. Hence the double meaning practised in all forms of underground literature. However, as well as pointing outwards in this way, wordplay always points inwards and refers to the duplicity of language itself. This is clearly dangerous territory. The *quiproquo*, one of the multifarious forms of punning,

[159] Porter, "Saving from the Wreck", 45.

[160] Walter Redfern, *Puns: Second Edition* (Harmondsworth: Penguin, 2000), 11.

can extend to a whole situation: a misreading as well as an alternative reading superimposed on reality.[161]

or

"... the unquestionable charm of the incorrect line".[162]

aussi

Redfern's description of wordplay doubles as a felicitous description for the methodology behind mistranslation and homophony in poetry. An overly self-conscious psychoanalytic version of this methodology—a *quiproquo* misreading of sorts—can also be found in Freud's "questionable" *re*-membering of "Signorelli", which was the name of an Italian artist whose name he wasn't able to recall while on a trip to Europe's so-called "subaltern", the Balkans. For Freud, the pun is a psychic release-valve in which humour alleviates the stress of repressing unpleasant truths.

He initially thought the painter's name was either "Botticelli" or "Boltraffio". That he couldn't remember the name, Freud claims, meant that he was suppressing a disturbing memory (in this case a former patient who suicided). Freud's unconscious had also attached to the memory a sexual content, which concealed itself through forgetting the name: "He had formed an unconscious association between the Italian painters and the Bosnians' valuing of sexual enjoyment over life".[163] Yet, despite his (unconscious?) espousing of cultural clichés, Freud reassembles his own "unconscious" processing of language remarkably well, as he often does, writing about these instances many years later and explaining the way puns work in his own repressed sexual desires—in this case, for the supposedly "pathological, anal, 'archaic', and in need of Oedipalization" Balkan other. He makes a connection between *Signorelli* and *Herzegovina* via *Signor* and *Herr*, both meaning "Sir". *Trafoi*, apparently the location he received news of the suicide, is linked to *Boltraffio*, while *Bosnia* was where the conversation took place, and *Botticelli*, a logical if naive final step:

[161] Redfern, *Puns: Second Edition*, 12.

[162] Mallarmé, *Divagations*, 201, my translation as opposed to Johnson's.

[163] Dušan I. Bjelić, "Balkan Geography and the De-Orientalization of Freud", *Journal of Modern Greek Studies* 29.1 (2011): 36.

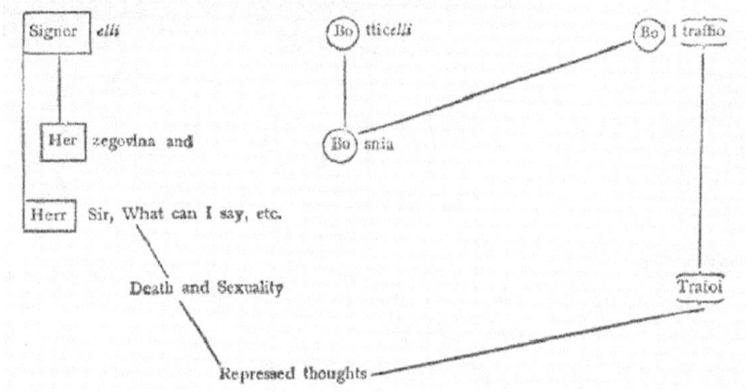

Fig. 18. Dušan I. Bjelić, Freud's Chemistry of Words (2011).

Yet Freud, in his analysis, also forgot to include the fact that he'd remembered seeing a picture of the painter Signorelli himself, found in the lower left corner of one of the painter's frescoes. The picture, a kind of signature, was therefore a third substitute to the forgotten name Signorelli. The "signature" can be interpreted as a reference to the Latin verb *signare* and this word, instead of Freud's *signore*, then leads us back to a simple analysis of the Signorelli parapraxis.[164] As would Freud's own name, *Sig*mund. The Bosnia-Herzegovina associations (*Bo* and *Herr*) that Freud himself introduced to bridge the gap between two failures of memory, are no longer necessary. As conscious as Freud is of his mind's movement through language, there are still slips he can't keep track of, voids he can't fill, proving by default his own hypothesis—that the unconscious thrives on the unreliably interchangeable structures of language. For Freud, the pun is also a subversive device whose tidiness enhances the illusion of self-mastery. So even when we don't believe a word he says, at least we can witness the stunning leaps, laps, lapses and lapsus in Freud's imaginative written accounts.[165]

[164] "Signorelli parapraxis", *Wikipedia*, which cites Huub Engels, *Emil Kraepelins Traumsprache 1908-1926* (2006): 66–9, https://en.wikipedia.org/wiki/Signorelli_parapraxis. This is the only source I could find.

[165] The "Signorelli" account first appears in 1901 in Freud, *The Psychopathology of Everyday Life*, Vol. 5 of the Pelican Freud Library, trans. Alan Tyson, 1960 (Harmondsworth: Penguin, 1975), 38–45.

aussi

The *quiproquo* wordplay methodology has its echo in Gregory Ulmer's coinage, the "puncept". In an anthology called *On Puns: The Foundation of Letters*, Ulmer illuminates the puncept at play in both Derrida's and Lacan's oeuvres, a Mallarméan/malleable use of the pun, shape-shifting across and re-shaping their ideas.[166] For a couple of *pat* instances that *tap* into this idea I'm trying to teethe/tease out, Lacan interchanges terms such as *dires* (sayings) and *désir* (desire), anagrams of each other, while Derrida champions the punning stunts in *Finnegans Wake* (read ahead for Derrida's *quiproquo* reading of Joyce via the Tower of Babel myth). At its core, the puncept is a methodology that "allows language to say what it knows, which allows the unconscious to show itself in the play of language".[167]

or

Another example is evident in Lacan's psychoanalytic concept of *jouissance* (bliss). Generally left untranslated to include the meaning of sexual orgasm, a *jouissance* drives the subject (similar to Freud's concept of the "death-drive") to repeatedly attempt to transgress the prohibitions, or err against the law, imposed on one's enjoyment—to go beyond the pleasure principle. But going beyond is also painful, and akin to Bataille's erotic philosophy, particularly as he refers to anguish ("when the bounds of the possible are over-reached, a recoil is inevitable"[168]), and as epitomised, here, in Lacan's mention (or "di-mention", an anglo-version of Derrida's *dit-mension*—another dimension opened up between the lines by "said" punning):

> Who does not know from experience that it is possible not to want to ejaculate? Who does not know from experience knowing the

[166] A separate though no less important example of punning that can shape and shift an oeuvre is embodied in one of Marcel Duchamp's pseudonyms, Rrose Sélavy. The name is a pun on the French phrase *Eros, c'est la vie*, which translates into English as "Eros, that's life". Duchamp signed written works with the name, and his cross-dressing alter ego allowed him to collaborate with Man Ray on a series of photographs. The pseudonym appeared in subsequent projects by other artists and writers, including in a collection of aphorisms, puns, and spoonerisms by the poet Robert Desnos.

[167] Gregory Ulmer, "The Puncept in Grammatology", in *On Puns: The Foundation of Letters*, ed. Jonathan Culler (Oxford: Basil Blackwell, 1988), 175.

[168] Bataille, *Eroticism*, 1962, trans. Mary Dalwood (London: Marion Boyars, 1987), 87.

> recoil imposed on everyone, in so far as it involves terrible promises, by the approach of *jouissance* as such. Who does not know that one may not wish to think?[169]

This last question places *jouissance* outside/beyond the Other (the Other being Lacan's definition of the unconscious, of language as symbolic structure), as Ulmer writes: "*Jouissance* refers, then, to a fourth sense, the four senses being sense, non-sense, common sense, and "*jouis*-sense'." The fifth sense (*jouis-sens* in French), "carries the insistence of desire in the chain of signifiers, productive of homonyms and puns".[170] This is the fifth dimension that homophonic translation flirts with, as di-mentioned above.

aussi

Mallarmé fondled the puncept in his *Crise de vers*, the crisis he also called a "liberation". He wrote of the "double state of speech" (or the "double state of the word" in most translations) and its place in the "the pure work" / "the book of verse" / "the Book of Books":

> An order innate to the book of verse exists inherently or everywhere, eliminating chance; it's also necessary, to eliminate the author: now, any subject is fated to imply, among the fragments brought together, a strange certainty about its appropriate place in the volume. It is susceptible to this because any cry possesses an echo—motifs of the same type balance each other, stabilizing each other at a distance, and neither the sublime incoherence of a romantic page, nor the artificial unity that adds up to a block-book, can provide it.[171]

In other words, "the book" is imaginary, unconscious, the Other: "Everything becomes suspense, a fragmentary disposition with alternations and oppositions, all working toward the total rhythm of the white spaces, which would be the poem silenced; but it is translated to some extent by each pendant. I want to consider it an instinct ..."[172]

[169] Lacan, *The Four Fundamental Conceptions of Psychoanalysis*, 1973, trans. Alan Sheridan (London: Hogarth, 1977), 234–5.

[170] Ulmer, "The Puncept in Grammatology", 175.

[171] Mallarmé, "Crisis of Verse", 208.

[172] Mallarmé, "Crisis of Verse", 209.

aussi

A pendant is an artistic composition intended to match or complement another. Given its meaning of a match or parallel, the pendant is also the pun. And wordplay *is* instinctive, requiring the poet to let loose their unconscious or disappear and, as Mallarmé would have it (and as noted a number of times already), "cede the initiative to words, set in motion by the clash of their inequalities". In homophonic translation, the poet can also *seed* the initiative to words, set in *com*motion by the clash of their *e*qualities.[173]

or

Is mistranslation any different to "translation", or to "writing"? There seem to be too many issues with the word "translation" itself for it to hold. Do we need new categories to add to those above, do we need other words for translation, or is the word translation simply splitting itself the way language and writing do?

aussi

While we're simultaneously deconstructing and reconstructing the dichotomies (and the many dimensions), we might as well construct a few separate categories for "mistranslation", or "versions":

1. Re-version — a re-membering of a poem, a post-Orphic coming back together.
2. Subversion — an undermining, a re-fragmentation, a return to the Underworld.
3. Aversion — a version to rid one's self of prior influence through textual annihilation.
4. Diversion — a version to distract, deviate, divert: be the deviant, be the clinamen!

[173] Incidentally, regarding puns: John Pollack, a former Clinton speechwriter and author of the book *The Pun Also Rises*, suggests that puns generally fell out of favour during the Enlightenment, when the form's reliance on imprecision and silliness was out of kilter with the prevailing spirit of sophistication and rational inquiry. See John Pollack, *The Pun Also Rises: How the Humble Pun Revolutionized Language, Changed History, and Made Wordplay More than Some Antics* (New York: Gotham, 2012).

5. Inversion — an upside-down version, a Down Under conceit: writing backwards through the original text to overturn the father, i.e. a *père*-version.[174]

or

Mallarmé proposes "Transposition; Structure, another", a notion that allows words, "through the clash of their inequalities", to "light each other up through reciprocal reflections", and which "gives you the surprise of never having heard that fragment of ordinary eloquence before … bathed in a brand new atmosphere".[175] Transposition, in Rasula and McCaffery, "is not a simple transit but a dichotomous zone of interaction"—interaction between languages, between aurality and visuality, between the imperfections of signs.[176]

or

To cite Mallarmé's *Crise de vers* again, this time at greater length:

> Languages imperfect insofar as they are many; the absolute one is lacking: thought considered as writing without accessories, not even whispers, still *stills* immortal speech; the diversity, on earth, of idioms prevents anyone from proferring words that would otherwise be, when made uniquely, the material truth. This prohibition is explicitly devastating, in Nature (one bumps up against it with a smile), where nothing leads one to take oneself for God; but, at times, turned toward aesthetics, my own sense regrets that discourse fails to express objects by touches corresponding to them in shading or bearing, since they do exist among the many languages, and sometimes in one.[177]

[174] Lacan's seminar XVII *L'envers de la psychanalyse*, *The Other Side of Psychoanalysis* (translated by another Australian, by the way) could now perhaps also be translated in this vein as *The Arse End of Analysis* or *Analysis Down Under*—a kind of per- or rather *père*-version, as Lacan himself says. See Lacan, *The Other Side of Psychoanalysis: The Seminar of Jacques Lacan, Book XVII*, trans. Russell Grigg (New York: W. W. Norton & Company, 2010). See also Toby Fitch, *The Bloomin' Notions of Other & Beau* (Marrickville: Vagabond Press, 2014), in which I write backwards through all of the *Illuminations* of Arthur Rimbaud.

[175] Mallarmé, "Crisis of Verse", 208–10.

[176] Rasula and McCaffery, *Imagining Language*, 203.

[177] Mallarmé, "Crisis of Verse", 205.

Mallarmé's crisis didn't stop him from thinking that poetry had the answers. He expounds that "*verse would not exist*" (his emphasis) but for this very untranslatability in Nature (as mentioned, he makes the point that the signified and the signifier in language rarely match—*nuit* is a bright sound, *jour* is dark), and that poetry, "philosophically, makes up for language's deficiencies, as a superior supplement". "[F]aced with the breaking up of classic literary rhythms … and their dispersion into articulated shivers close to instrumentation" (remember the vibrations of strange attractors) Mallarmé heralds poetry's ability to *transpose* itself into new forms for new eras, "for an art of achieving the transposition into the Book of the symphony…"[178]

or

Is verse, or poetry, truly better than any other use of language in translating Nature (or the real, as representation), even if poetry can be symphonic? Poetry, despite its complex aural, visual, musical, multilingual capabilities, is still restricted by systems of language; it's still a construct, fabrication, go-between, chimera, shadow. Perhaps poetry is just more open to shape-shifting, to being other (and multiple, polyvalent) in its search for other forms.

aussi

While Mallarmé gifts us the term "transposition", Derrida writes, in *Positions*—a book of three interviews that translate some of his more complex concepts into a more accessible form—of how translation could do with another definition, a substitute: "In the limits to which it is possible, or at least *appears* possible, translation practices the difference between signified and signifier. But if this difference is never pure, no more so is translation, and for the notion of translation we would have to substitute a notion of *transformation*: a regulated transformation of one language by another, of one text by another."[179]

In other words, the problematic difference between signifier and signified is doubled in translation. "Transformation" as definition goes a step further than Mallarmé's "transposition" in relating the mutational aspects of writing.

[178] Mallarmé, "Crisis of Verse", 205–6 and 210.
[179] Derrida, *Positions*, 20.

aussi

Most conversations about translation evoke the story of the Tower of Babel from the Book of Genesis, a story that "is always in our interest ... to reread closely."[180] In *The Ear of the Other*, Derrida writes of "the great challenge to translation", *Finnegans Wake*, for its multilingual punning methodology. In "The Puncept in Grammatology", Ulmer quotes first David Hayman and then Umberto Eco, who identify the "principal lesson" of *Finnegans Wake*:

> "The *Wake* belongs to a class (not a genre) of works which invite the reader to perpetuate creation". Eco agrees: "The search for 'open' models capable of guaranteeing and founding the mutation and the growth and, finally, the vision of a universe founded on possibility, as contemporary philosophy and science suggest to the imagination, encounters perhaps its most provoking and violent representation—perhaps its anticipation—in *Finnegans Wake*".[181]

Derrida describes how a Babelian motif runs from one end of the book to the other (the book, of course, is circular, with the last sentence only being completed by the incomplete opening sentence). Derrida picks out the moment in *Finnegans Wake* when Yahweh interrupts the construction of the tower by the tribe of the Shems[182] to condemn humanity to a multiplicity of languages—"which is to say, to the necessary and impossible task of translation". In that moment in *Finnegans Wake*, the three words "*And he war*" appear.[183] "In what language is this written?" Derrida asks, then continues:

> despite the multiplicity of languages, cultural references, and condensations, English is indisputably the dominant language in

[180] Derrida, "Roundtable on Translation", 100. George Steiner's *After Babel*, most importantly, is a comprehensive study of translation which deals with the "Babel problem" of multiple languages. See Steiner, *After Babel: Aspects of Language and Translation* (Oxford: Oxford University Press, 1975).

[181] Ulmer, "The Puncept in Grammatology", 171.

[182] "The tribe of the Shems" is Derrida's terminology, not Joyce's. Derrida stresses that their name, *Shem*, already means "name" in Hebrew.

[183] James Joyce, *Finnegans Wake* (Harmondsworth: Penguin, 1999), 258. It mustn't be forgotten that, despite its multilingual punning stunts, *Finnegans Wake* should also be viewed as being written in Irish English as a subversion of the hegemony of the English language.

> *Finnegans Wake*—all these refractions and slippages are produced in English or through English, in the body of that language. French would translate the English as: *il-guerre* (he wars), he declares war. And that's indeed what happens: God declares war on the tribe of the Shems who want to make a name for themselves by raising the tower and imposing their tongue on the universe. But obviously the German word *war* influences the English word, so we also have: He was, he was the one who said, for example, "I am that I am", which is the definition of Yahweh. And then one also hears the ear, which is very present in the rest of the text. *One hears a thousand things through other languages* (my emphasis).[184]

Derrida describes how translation cannot mark "the fact there are, in one linguistic system, perhaps several languages or tongues". So then, if it is always in our interest to re-read this story closely, the Tower of Babel is surely a reminder story of a reminder story, as humanity continually needs reminding of the plurality of languages and the plurality *within* languages. Babel is the name that God imposes on the tower and the Shems. Babel is itself the name of the father, therefore God is imposing his own name on the Shems, which, when they come to translate it, can "confusedly be understood as confusion". Derrida continues: "Babel equals Confusion. This is the paradigm of the situation in which there is a multiplicity of languages and in which translation is both necessary and impossible".

By imposing his untranslatable name which must be translated, God produces what Derrida calls a "disschemination", which has at least four senses: dissemination, deschematization, de-"Shemitizing", and derouting or diverting from a path (the word *chemin* meaning path or road); and which forces the Shems into a position of "Translate me and what is more don't translate me".[185]

[184] Derrida, "Roundtable on Translation", 98–9.
[185] Derrida, "Roundtable on Translation", 102–3.

or

BABBLE.

aussi

With so many double/treble/quadruple entendres in the story of the Tower of Babel, it would seem that translation, "necessary and impossible", is actually—always and already—mistranslation. According to Derrida, even the word for tongue is mistranslated. The Hebrew word signifies "lip", so the Shems in fact desire to impose their lip on the universe.[186]

or

Perhaps hoping to enact the inverse of the Shems—Brennan, Edwards and Tranter give the French Euroverse some Down Under lip.

or

After such a babbling anecdote, it might now be argued that homophonic mistranslation attempts the inverse of translation (at the same time as a "literal" sound/phonetic translation), in that it teases out "several languages or tongues" already in the one linguistic system. Homophonic mistranslation attempts to subvert or invert the hierarchy of one language over another by transforming the sounds of one linguistic system (and its many tongues) into sounds from another linguistic system (and its many tongues). (Remember, in both Edwards and Tranter, we're reading an Australian English, replete with its many colloquial tongues, subverting the mother tongue first of all, while also subverting the literary French.) In a homophonic mistranslation, every word becomes a little tongue looping between languages—a complex interaction of soundplay, a methodology seen and heard in *Finnegans Wake*.

[186] Derrida, "Roundtable on Translation", 101.

or

As Random Cloud writes of *Wake*, linking the pun to an erotic multiplicity, and to an everlasting destruction of singularity in language: "James Joyce conceived of *Finnegans Wake* as a circe, a simultanus short-circuit of all myth (Every Thing Equally and Immediately Remote), an indefinitely wyrm-edened book—in a word, an apoca*lapse*".[187]

Fig. 19. Theodoros Pelecanos, drawing of an ouroboros (1478).

aussi

After all, a "fluke" is a tremotode worm, a parasite.[188] Writhing round.

[187] Random Cloud, "Fearful Assymetry", in *The Cambridge Companion to Textual Scholarship*, ed. Neil Fraistat and Julia Flanders (Cambridge: Cambridge University Press, 2013), 164. Note the puns, and in particular the word "simultanus", its "*or*-play", its homoerotic tail overlapping, enfolding into its tongue, and its desire, like any pun, to have it both ways, simultaneously.

[188] Edwards, "Double Talk".

or

With its tail between its legs, or rather its lips, the tower of Babel, allegorically, is a phallic symbol brought down by a declaration of non-independence, of plurality and multiplicity—by, simultaneously, a circulation (a re-insertion into itself) and a "disschemination".

7

Fig. 20. Caravaggio, *Head of Medusa* (1597).

In an interview with *Poetry International Web*, Chris Edwards writes/speaks about the reasons he returned to poetry after twenty years underground, not publishing any poetry, undergoing his own *crise de vers.* He cites Hélène Cixous's critique of phallocentrism as a vital influence in his poetic revival, and at length:

> Hélène Cixous's essay (or polemic, or manifesto) "The Laugh of the Medusa" revived, or revised, my interest in poetry in the early 1990s. "Nearly the entire history of writing," she wrote, "is confounded with the history of reason, of which it is the effect, the support and one of the privileged alibis. It has been one with the phallocentric tradition. It is indeed that same self-admiring, self-stimulating, self-congratulatory phallocentrism." "There have," however, "been poets who would go to any lengths to slip something by at odds with tradition … But only the poets—not the novelists, allies of representationalism. Because poetry involves gaining strength through the unconscious and because the unconscious, that other limitless country, is the place where the repressed manage to survive: women, or as Hoffman would say, fairies." Cixous called for volcanic upheaval, seeing in women and poets alike a "capacity to depropriate unselfishly", producing "a whole composed of parts that are wholes, not simple partial objects but a moving, limitlessly changing ensemble, a cosmos tirelessly traversed by Eros, an immense astral space not organised around any one sun that's any more of a star than the others."[189]

aussi

Australian poet-scholar David Musgrave characterises Edwards' and Tranter's versions of Mallarmé as a repetition of Brennan's modernist crisis:

> Both poets seem compelled to repeat the performative nature of Brennan's engagement with Mallarmé as a tribute to his fitful, originary gesture towards literary modernism. In this regard, their works enact a nostalgia for a lost state or a city that never existed: a kind of modernist Paris situated as the symbolic and imaginary capital of an avant-garde, post-colonial poetic enterprise which only came into being belatedly in the Australian tradition.[190]

[189] Edwards, "Interview with Chris Edwards".

[190] David Musgrave, "Paris, Capital of the Australian Poetic Avant-Garde: Christopher Brennan's 'Musicopoematographoscope', John Tranter's 'Desmond's Coupé' and Chris Edwards' 'A Fluke' and *After Naptime*", in Alistair Rolls, ed. *Remembering Paris: Echoes of Baudelaire in Text and on Screen* (Bristol and Chicago: Intellect, 2021), 182.

And while this is apt in traditional understandings of literary lineage or inheritance, and in an Australian poetic avant-garde context frequently cited as "belated" in global and canonistic terms,[191] the analysis falls short of acknowledging the distinct personal poetic crises of Edwards and Tranter (both filtered albeit through French forebears) and the attempts, especially in Edwards, to use form and the abject to dissolve binaries (of self and other, of subject and object) and boundaries (of person and nation, of the present and the epochal). Another take on Paris as colonial alternative to the motherland can be found in Farrell, who suggests: "[The French] might have been our Imperial Masters, but weren't, cocking a snook at those who were. Colin Dyer writes of the French (who admittedly behaved dismally elsewhere) and Australia: 'They came and they saw, but they made no attempt to conquer.' Summarily, the English gave us poetic tradition, but the French showed us how to be modern."[192] It is less interesting to continue to frame such poetics by reasserting categorical borders, when the poetry is clearly asking us not to always be so faithful to them, temporally, aesthetically, conceptually, and is otherwise insisting we consider its multiplicity as "a whole composed of parts that are wholes … a moving, limitlessly changing ensemble".

[191] See the aforementioned Carruthers on Brennan.

[192] Farrell, "Rebellious Tropes".

or

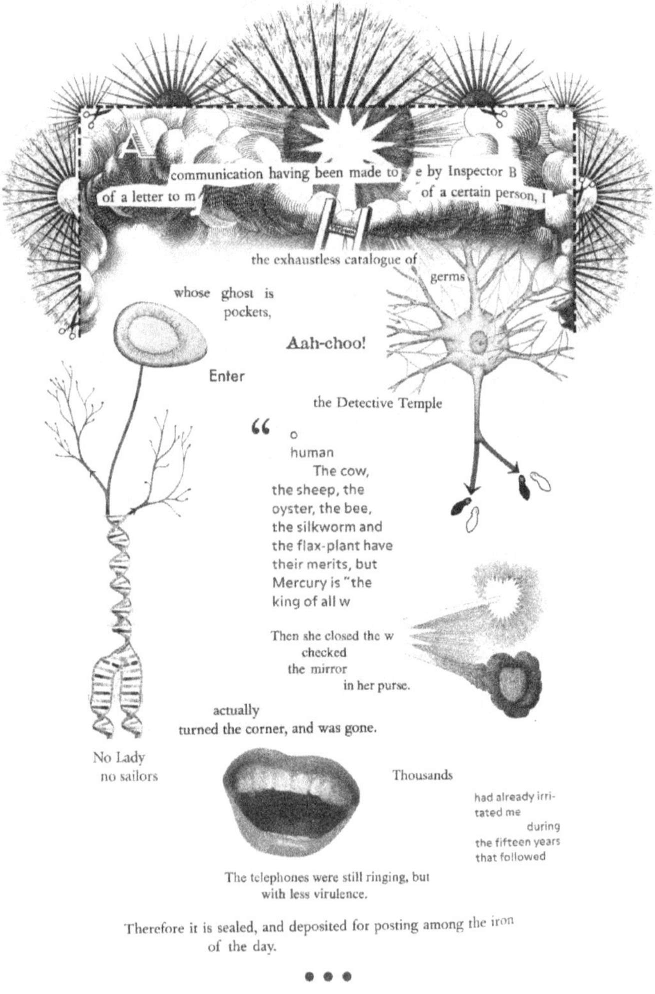

Fig. 21. The first (single) page of Chris Edwards' *After Naptime* (2014), 7.

One of Edwards' subsequent books, *After Naptime: A Poem, Profusely Illustrated* (2014), is an expansion of this (w)holey project. It's a two-Act drama—with a Preface and an Interregnum to introduce the "story", and an Intermission (that isn't really a pause), followed by a Coda. And in an explicit development of *Un Coup de dés* and "A Fluke", its facing pages are treated as a single theatrical spread—a single stage—"with centrally located orchestra pit".[193] The poem is also a "mined / over / matter"[194] assemblage. In the back of the book, there's a spooky list of sources for the poem's fragments of text and profuse use of images, sources Edwards "mined" (whole) snippets from to (re)assemble in a new ensemble using old-fashioned cut-and-paste methods (but with a scanner and software as scissors and glue). These sources include Dennis Cooper's "The Anal-Retentive Line Editor", Charles Dickens' *Bleak House* and *David Copperfield*, a book on muscle building, *The Myths of Greece and Rome*, a book on DNA, *The Penguin Book of Ghost Stories*, some newspaper articles, a book on alchemy and mysticism, and a Maigret mystery by Georges Simenon, among others. As one would expect from this kind of project, there's no "unitary meaning", but what emerges is the autobiography "of a certain person, I / the exhaustless catalogue of germs / whose ghost is pockets // Aah-choo!"[195]

aussi

The facing pages in *After Naptime* are collage couples, as understood in late nineteenth-century Parisian slang—not formally united, but inseparable (remember, *coller* means "to paste, stick, glue", while *collage* is slang for an illicit sexual union): "Like any other couple, they fight, flirt, ignore one another, interrupt one another, trade insults or endearments, finish each other's sentences, trade observations and rejoinders, and so on."[196]

[193] Edwards, *After Naptime*, quoted from the back cover blurb.

[194] Edwards, *After Naptime* (Marrickville: Vagabond Press, Stray Dog Editions, 2014), 16.

[195] Edwards, *After Naptime*, 8.

[196] Chris Edwards and Toby Fitch, "*After Naptime* Launch Interview", Vagabond Xmas Party, Gleebooks, Sydney, December 7, 2014.

or

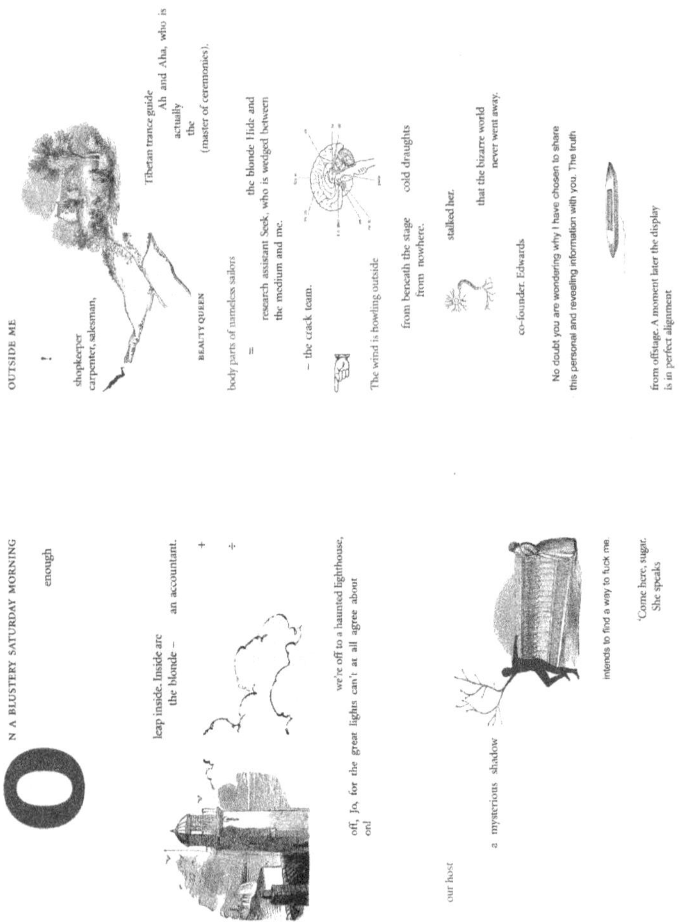
ON A BLUSTERY SATURDAY MORNING

enough

leap inside. Inside are
the blonde – an accountant.

+

÷

we're off to a haunted lighthouse,
off, Jo, for the great lights can't at all agree about
on!

our host

a mysterious shadow

intends to find a way to fuck me.

'Come here, sugar.
She speaks

OUTSIDE ME

!

shopkeeper
carpenter, salesman,

Tibetan trance guide
Ah and Aha, who is
actually
the
(master of ceremonies).

BEAUTY QUEEN

body parts of nameless sailors

=

research assistant Seek, who is wedged between
the medium and me.
the blonde I hide and

– the crack team.

The wind is howling outside

from beneath the stage cold draughts
from nowhere.

stalked her.

that the bizarre world
never went away.

co-founder, Edwards

No doubt you are wondering why I have chosen to share
this personal and revealing information with you. The truth

from offstage. A moment later the display
is in perfect alignment

Fig. 22. A double-page spread from *After Naptime*, 10–11.

One of the first icons in the constellations of text and image, and a nod to the shipwreck in *Un Coup de dés*, is a lighthouse,[197] possibly extracted from one particular source—a *Sydney Morning Herald Good Weekend* magazine article with a Ghostbusters ring to it—"Who You Gonna Call?" by John van Tiggelen. The article describes a trip to a haunted lighthouse with a team of paranormal investigators called Hide and Seek, one of whom happens to have the surname Edwards. The lighthouse is also a phallic symbol, in this case ejaculating a beam of light (or enlightenment?), and because it resembles a capital "I" it could stand in for "I", consciousness in general, and identity, too, even if that's not the same thing. It's also a haunted lighthouse, a consciousness troubled by ghosts—uncertainties, undecidabilities if you like—being investigated by a team of people, one of them Edwards—and as such becomes a tongue-in-cheek phallic figure, and a pendant (like the words that are pendants, complementing them, acting metonymically), but also a conduit for the emission of an ambiguous, amorphous multiple languaged self.

or

In a performative, scripted interview I conducted with Edwards at *After Naptime*'s book launch, I asked Edwards a question about the influence of Freud and psychoanalysis on his use of imagery in *After Naptime*, and quoted Liz Grosz—"there is … no logic outside that … given by the phallus; there is no identity other than that given by the phallus"—to which Edwards replied:

> As Freud sees it, male genitalia are "wholes" *with* a "w", female genitalia holes *without* a "w". You either have or lack the phallus, and your psyche revolves around that. Luce Irigaray tried to think otherwise in *This Sex Which Is Not One*, back in the seventies, and her ideas contributed to the form of *After Naptime*. Irigaray contrasts "the one of form, of the individual, of the (male) sex organ" with "the contact of at least two (lips)" that "keeps woman in touch with herself." She describes a sexuality that is always at least double—

[197] There's also an image of a shipwreck that more directly alludes to the "Naufrage" of *Un Coup de dés*, and perhaps even to the "Damn" of Brennan's "Musicopoematographoscope".

> though it goes further, she says, and is plural—and a subjectivity that is multiple, diffuse and tactile.[198]

Edwards' lighthouse, haunted by undecidables, enlightens us of his critique of a singular self, gender, consciousness or identity ("ON A BLUSTERY MORNING // OUTSIDE ME", "Unfortunately me / I mean, we", and "I was / gifts / of either gender"[199]), while the "holes" (the blank spaces on the page) between the "wholes" (fragments of text and images) become, or are becoming of, Edwards' troubling of any self-admiring, self-stimulating, self-congratulatory phallocentrism (as Cixous characterised "the history of reason" in literature). With all these (w)-holes, Edwards' "identification" with "fairies", plural, comes to fruition in lines like: "our host // a shadow // intends to find a way to fuck me", or, read across the double-page spread, "The truth // intends to find a way to fuck me".[200]

[198] Edwards and Fitch. "*After Naptime* Launch Interview".
[199] Edwards, *After Naptime*, 10–11, 18 and 9.
[200] Edwards, *After Naptime*, 10–11.

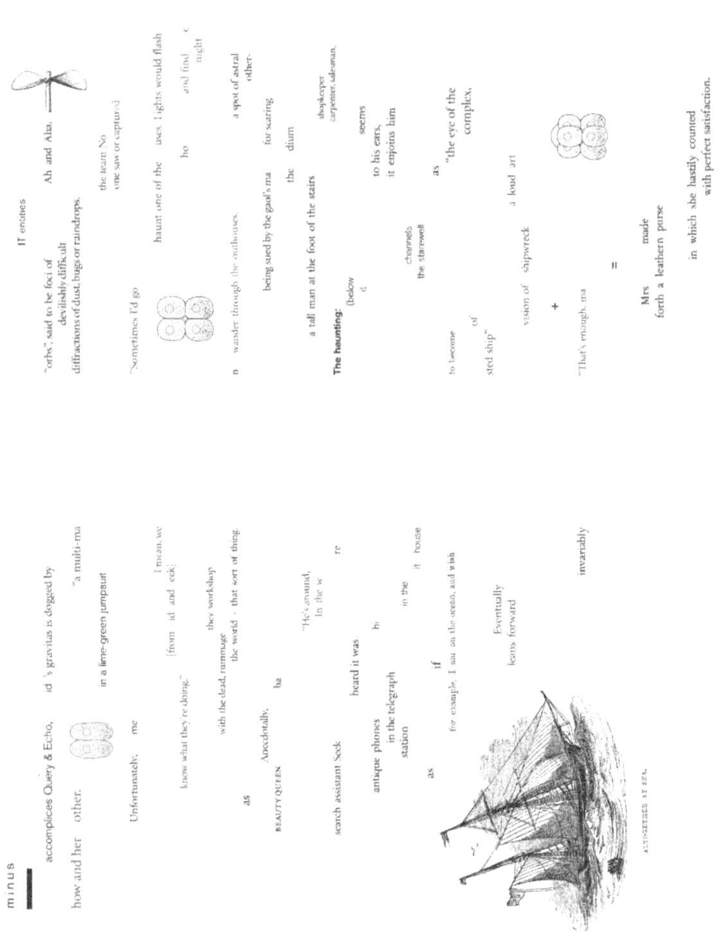

Fig. 23. A double-page spread from *After Naptime*, 18–19.

aussi

Musgrave astutely sees how Edwards' images form emblems with the surrounding text, similar to emblem books (popular in Europe from the fifteenth to the eighteenth centuries). He zooms in on the most prevalent image, the nerve cell, "a significant motif in at least two senses":

> it is an emblem of networking, or communicability, and could be taken to be an icon of intertextuality; it is also an emblem of discharge, for the nerve cell functions, physiologically speaking, through a rise in electric potential which then leads to a discharge of current that allows transmission of the nerve impulse. In this latter sense, each image of dendrite, synapse and axon is metonymic of the discharges that are typographically dispersed through the *livre composé*: "Ahchoo!" It can be argued then that one unifying strand of the book is the orgasm, taken not only literally but also symbolically: in Lacanian psychoanalytic terms, it is a *jouissance*, or an excess which has no use value; but equally it could be seen to evoke Roland Barthes' notion of *jouissance* as the pleasure of being lost in the text.[201]

or

As Edwards writes, fully parodying the orgasmic futility of self, representation and self-representation that is conjured in this work:

> that fragment of text when I found it—"Aah-choo!"—I don't remember where, exactly—seemed haunted to me by an Egyptian myth, or at least by a sliver of one. The first god, you see, was Atum, who was simultaneously male and female. Atum was alone and had nothing to do except sit on the Ben-ben mound in the middle of Nun, the dark waters. So, as you do, Atum masturbated. But when Atum tasted and swallowed the resulting seed, Atum couldn't help coughing and sneezing. The coughing produced Tefnut (moisture), and the sneezing produced Shu (air). These gods, Shu and Tefnut, were alternately male and female, so they coupled to produce the next generation. Shu became, in my mind at least, the archaic ghost or double of "Aah-choo!" Shu is Air sneezed by Atum—a sneeze

[201] Musgrave, "Paris, Capital of the Australian Poetic Avant-Garde", 178.

> bursting from a god, a god bursting from a sneeze. To this, "Aah-choo!" adds what Jacques Derrida calls in his collage book *Glas* "the element of contagion, the infinite circulation of general equivalence" that "relates each sentence, each stump of writing … to each other."[202]

or

Jacques Rancière describes the crisis in verse at the end of the nineteenth century, the dispersing of the French alexandrine: "The poet no longer has a model, celestial or human, to imitate. Henceforth, it is by the mere 'dialectic of verse' that [they] will be able to revivify the seal of the idea, by forging together, according to an essential rhythm, 'many scattered veins of ore, unknown and floating'."[203]

While there might not have been poetic models worth imitating, because the models had grown stale (needing "disschemination"), there was a renewed need for "forgery" (Mallarmé uses the English word)—to forge together new forms.

aussi

Considering these Australian "versions" and extrapolations of *Un Coup de dés*, perhaps now, in the twenty-first century, after all the fragmentation of the twentieth, there is a growing desire for new forgeries to catch on—to rejoin with rejoinders of the "cosmos tirelessly traversed by Eros"—aware that there could only be such forgeries by experimentation with forms both interconnected *and* fragmented (networked and contagious as poems are, within and without). As Edwards can visualise:

> I like the idea of treating Australian poems, including Ern Malley's, not as dot-like entities (e.g. lyrics) or sites of authorial self-presence (meaning in isolation), but as string-like (there's that lyre again) interwoven filaments—nodes, if you like, in a worldwide network of sociocultural webs (meaning as oscillation and experimental flux).[204]

[202] Edwards and Fitch. "*After Naptime* Launch Interview".

[203] Jacques Rancière, quoting from *Mallarmé's critical prose poem* "Solemnity", in *Mallarmé: The Politics of the Siren*, trans. Steve Corcoran (London: Continuum, 2011), 11.

[204] Edwards, "Interview with Chris Edwards".

At the heart of this statement are the impossible, the invisible, and the plural—the many ineffables that the poem seeks to mine and forge into something that oscillates between the decidable and the undecidable, between the known and the unknown, beyond borders, between and beyond ears/eras, perhaps even beyond the planetary, certainly the "universal". As Rancière concludes, quoting Mallarmé's *La musique et les lettres*: "Poetry is meditation, doubt transformed into hyperbole and that which 'projects, to a great forbidden and thunderous height, our conscious lack of what, up there, gleams'. One can say that this projection is a deception (*supercherie*) or forgery. But the forgery is also the work done by a goldsmith in 'sowing doubt with rubies'."[205]

or

A homophonic translation hyperbolises the doubt of "our conscious lack of what, up there, gleams", and "our unconscious lock on what, down here, gleans". Homophony hangs on the split dualities of words, highlighting the signifier, dispersing the signified, while collapsing the ground beneath both, i.e. sowing doubt with rubies. Where Mallarmé's chains of suggestion intertwine and coalesce, increasing in power as we trace them across his oeuvre, a mistranslation's network of suggestion, contagious, spreads across platforms and places, across eras, and, erotically, across multiple authors.

or

"[E]very word or letter I looked at was suggestive, and it wasn't always easy to remain *faithful* to all of them at once" (my emphasis).[206]

or

Un Coup de dés becomes exactly what its oscillating poetics designed it to become: an ALSO-MACHINE, generating genomes, liminal looms, fantastical phantasms, altered alternatives, *other* others, *aussi* Aussies.

[205] Rancière, *Mallarmé: The Politics of the Siren*, 22.
[206] Edwards, "Double Talk".

aussi

For all Mallarmé's spouting of the *oeuvre pure*, the "search for the One Book all poets are attempting to write", he may well have spawned *the One Poem all books are attempting to write. Un Coup de dés* and its musical imagery, its vast landscape visuals and blank spaces on the page, its seductive gutter-traversing, its untouchable lack of meaning locked into correspondence with the Other, its (mis)rendered thought disseminated as indeterminate fragments—and, above all, its *multi-nefarious* "and/or" poetics, its self-positioning as dumbfounded Master in a foundered ship—have created some of the most perfect preconditions for a mistranslation storm, and for transformation in a broader formal sense. Infinitely reproducible, a poem for endless spelunking, a spectre to haunt the haunted, the mobile to hang over the skyline and join the constellations. Storm clouds sneezing on the horizon. This is its great modernist haunting:

CONSIDERED A LOST CAUSE AMID CIRCUMSTANTANTIAL /

EVERLASTING INTESTINAL SPASMS //

WOULD OFFER YOU UP A LIKE SHIPWRECK ...[207]

or

The best modern literature, says Kristeva, explores the place of the abject, a place where boundaries crumble, where we are confronted with an archaic space before such linguistic binaries as self and other, subject and object. The transcendent and sublime, for Kristeva, are simply our attempts at covering over the breakdowns (and subsequent reassertion of boundaries) associated with the abject: "On close inspection, all literature is probably a version of the apocalypse that seems to me rooted, no matter what its sociohistorical conditions might be, on the fragile border (borderline cases) where identities (subject/object, etc.) do not exist or only barely so—double, fuzzy, heterogeneous, animal, metamorphosed, altered, abject".[208]

[207] Edwards, "A Fluke", 43.

[208] Kristeva, *Powers of Horror*, 207.

or

Such literature spelunks the cave, the lack, the want, that language is structured around. Kristeva elevates poetry in this regard because of its willingness to play with and break apart grammar, metaphor and meaning—because such poems "compel language to come nearest to the human enigma, to the place where it kills, thinks, and experiences jouissance all at the same time. A language of abjection of which the writer is both subject[209] and victim, witness and topple. Toppling into what? Into nothing …"[210]

A literature of the void, I would say, but not just Mallarmé's. I'm thinking of Edwards' [N]EVER [N]EVER. In its "double, fuzzy, heterogeneous, animal, metamorphosed, altered, abject" rigadoon with *Un Coup de dés*, "A Fluke" exhibits, in its own words, the "laughter of the apocalypse". Its surface play, subjective but ambivalent attitude, its suspended exclamations and absurdity, its gushing forth of the unconscious, repressed desire, and suppressed pleasure—lays bear the fact that language is at once contingent, arbitrary, shipwrecked and limned with the abject fear of loss. Or, as Kristeva writes: "Not a language of the desiring exchange of messages or objects that are transmitted in a social contract of communication and desire beyond want, but a language of want, of the fear that edges up to it and runs along its edges".[211]

or

An apoca*lapse* lapping at Australian shores.

[209] To clarify, through these various theories—some from the philosophies of deconstruction and some from science and psychoanalysis and elsewhere—I'm not arguing that subjectivity can be erased and I'm not advocating for the erasure of the other; quite the opposite, in fact. I'm arguing that the techniques used in mistranslations can be augmented to subvert hegemonic structures within literature and, ergo, its role in representing those structures in the world. See the next, final subchapter, for a treatment of the political implications of these literary strategies regarding settler Australia.

[210] Kristeva, *Powers of Horror*, 206.

[211] Kristeva, *Powers of Horror*, 38.

8

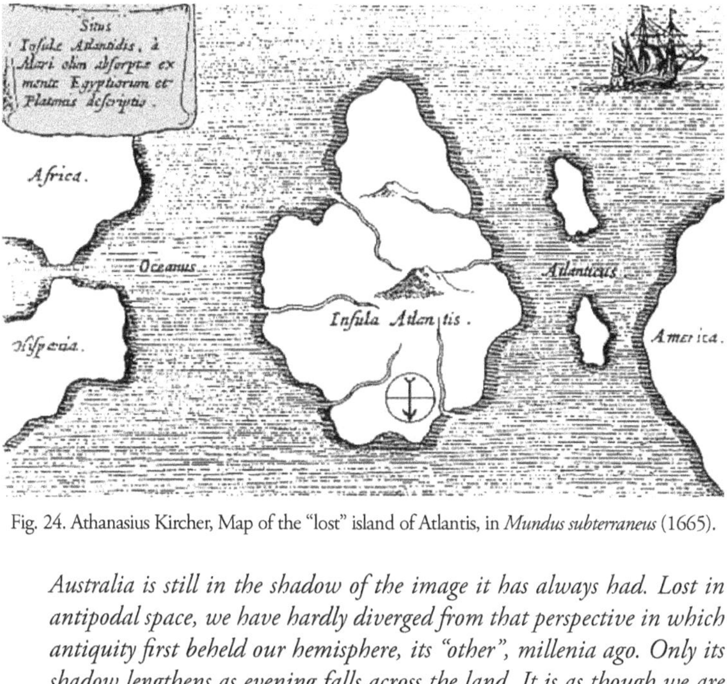

Fig. 24. Athanasius Kircher, Map of the "lost" island of Atlantis, in *Mundus subterraneus* (1665).

> *Australia is still in the shadow of the image it has always had. Lost in antipodal space, we have hardly diverged from that perspective in which antiquity first beheld our hemisphere, its "other", millenia ago. Only its shadow lengthens as evening falls across the land. It is as though we are endlessly absorbed by it, into it. Whence that wasted prospect in our eyes. Our deserts, desolation, desertion. That country constantly reflecting on its own revolving.*[212] —Paul Foss

Plato's Atlantis—that mythical antipodean land of potential abun*dance* and treasures, that piece of *pure invention* invaded and conquered by European colonial expansion—turned out to be "Australia", a country

[212] Paul Foss, "Theatrum Nondum Cognitorum", in *Foreign Bodies Papers*, eds. Peter Botsman, Chris Burns and Peter Hutchings (Sydney: Local Consumption Publications, 1981), 17.

populated not by a great white race who would create huge trade, but by over 500 nations of Aborigines who had lived on and knew intimately the multiple landscapes of the continent. Yet, since it was "discovered", a discourse of the void and its related imagery resounds through its colonial literature, from the early explorers who described *Terra Australis* as a wasteland,[213] to the "whitewashing" of Australian history, as if First Nations peoples could simply be banished into the void (as viewed from the invaders' perspective) from whence they appeared.[214] The dispossession of the first Australians "underwrote the development of the nation" and over two hundred years would pass before the High Court of Australia rejected the fiction that when Australia was discovered it was *terra nullius*—nobody's land—and rather recognised that Indigenous peoples have native title: land rights that existed before the British invaded and which can still exist today.[215]

aussi

Justin Clemens and Thomas H. Ford have recently shown that the imposition of *terra nullius* in Australia was linked to the invention of the nation itself by a (bad) poet who made puns on his own name—Barron Field, a poet of the Master. In 1817, as the new Judge of the Supreme Court of Civil Judicature in New South Wales—the highest legal authority in the colonised land—Field appropriated the official government printer to self-publish the first *book* of poems ever printed on the continent,[216] his own *First Fruits of Australian Poetry* (1819), written

[213] Paul Foss writes: "From William Jansz of the *Duyfken* (1606) to Cook of the Endeavour (1770), and beyond, the antipodal simulacrum is draped over the country like a shroud. It is still hear here, haunting the present with its echoes". For descriptive quotes of the "wasteland" that Australia's "discoverers" encountered, see Foss, "Theatrum Nondum Cognitorum", 31–3.

[214] For an example of the ongoing revisionism of Australian history regarding the dispossession of Indigenous land, see Robert Manne, ed., Whitewash: On Keith *Windschuttle's Fabrication of Aboriginal History* (Collingwood: Black Inc., 2003). For an analysis on two major narratives of Indigenous dispossession in Australian history (native title and the Stolen Generations), see Bain Attwood, "Unsettling pasts: reconciliation and history in settler Australia", *Postcolonial Studies* 8.3 (2015): 243–59, http://dx.doi.org/10.1080/13688790500231012.

[215] See "Mabo v Queensland", No. 2, HCA 23, 175 CLR 1 (June 3, 1992).

[216] Other verse had recently been published in the colony. Michael Massey Robinson, shipped out as a convict because of his attempts at extortion, and who later, coincidentally, became a lawyer and one of the original shareholders of the Bank of New South Wales, is regarded as the first published writer of verse in Australia, with his 20 patriotic odes

under the Romantic influence of his poet friends back in the mother country, William Wordsworth, Charles Lamb and Leigh Hunt. It is claimed that Field was one of the first to even use the term "Australia" in a poem (albeit rhyming it with "failure") in 1819, when the term wasn't yet in common use until the late 1820s.[217]

In just two poems, one about monstrous flora ("Botany-Bay Flowers") and one about a metaphorical monster ("The Kangaroo"), Field's *First Fruits* is a deliberate plundering of the field of poetry, and a bold attempt, bound up in legal fabrications, to create "Australian poetry", and thus, through language, "Australia" (where he saw no existing language structures worthy of his appropriations). Because, at the same time he was publishing this entrepreneurial work of poetry, Field was also influencing the law: "Asked to determine whether Governor Macquarie had authority to impose taxes in the colony, Field issued a fateful judgement that established, for the first time, what [would later be] called *terra nullius*."[218] To avoid having to pay taxes, he determined that the colony of NSW was governed by Parliament, not the Crown, because it was unoccupied—"there could be no owners nor agriculture in the country before [its] settlement".[219] Using his colonial position of power, he embedded all this in poetic language. The concept of *terra nullius* appears presciently in Field's punning on his own name "Barron Field" ("and what barren plains"[220]), a depropriation of his first name from noun to adjective and a decharacterisation of his surname from "field" to the general "plain". As "a personage who claims that there are, as yet, no local sources from which and about which he can write",[221] he virtually plagiarises the canon

published in the Sydney Gazette between 1810 and 1820, and then altogether on three sides of a large folder. See Donovan Clarke, "Michael Massey Robinson", in Australian Dictionary of Biography, Vol. 2, 1967, and online 2006, https://adb.anu.edu.au/biography/robinson-michael-massey-2598.

217 Australia was commonly called New Holland at the time. See David Brooks, "Field's Kangaroo", *Kenyon Review* (March/April 2017): 29–43.

218 See Justin Clemens and Thomas H. Ford, *Barron Field in New South Wales: The Poetics of Terra Nullius* (Melbourne: Melbourne University Press, 2023).

219 Clemens, "First Fruits of a Barron Field", *Critical Quarterly* (May 14, 2019): 32, https://doi.org/10.1111/criq.12451.

220 See "Botany-Bay Flowers" in Barron Field, *First Fruits of Australian Poetry* (Sydney: Printed by George Howe, 1819). Barron Field, *First Fruits*, 2nd edition (Sydney: Printed by R. Howe, 1823), 1.

221 Clemens, "First Fruits of a Barron Field", 21.

as he received it from the motherland, obsessively alluding to or directly appropriating Lucretius, Shakespeare, Joseph Hall, John Milton, John Dryden, Aristotle, Juvenal, Pliny the Elder, Wordsworth, and Coleridge, and, by doing so, projecting their words on to his formulation of the colony.[222] The title *First Fruits*, also, becomes a knowing satire of his tax evasion, which relied on the assertion that if the land was unoccupied it was also void of agriculture (in spite of the evidence of Aborigines using sophisticated techniques including, among others, fire-stick farming to manage vegetation, cultivate crops and facilitate hunting, and their growing of tubers for Yams in a way that allowed for them to be regrown the next season).

There is an obvious irony to Field, as self-appointed impresario of Australian poetry, implanting in his "apoems or … faux-po"[223] barren puns on his own name that render him and his poetry synonymous with the settler view of the land as void, as nobody's, as a blank page to be filled with the Master's language, legal and poetic. Unable to escape his own subjectivity as a Romantic wannabe, poetic kleptomaniac and judge concocting laws to justify invasion, he splits his own "unfabulous" body (of work): "he is himself the incompetent mixed metaphor of which he speaks in his verses: a split subject, split in and by his encounter with the land".[224]

aussi

Field's poem "The Kangaroo", in its desire for national identity-formation, is almost an autobiographical blazon—not only satirising the split subject of his poetic identity metaphorically as a hybrid creature, but also his vision of "Australia" as a strange new "barren" body to inhabit (physically and in language):

> Kanagaroo, Kangaroo!
> Thou Spirit of Australia,
> That redeems from utter failure,
> From perfect desolation,

[222] Even Charles Lamb, at the time, described Field's book as an "inauspicious unliterary Thiefland". See Charles Lamb, "Review of Barron Field, *First Fruits of Australian Poetry* (1819)", *Examiner*, January 16, 1820, 39.

[223] Clemens, "First Fruits of a Barron Field", 32.

[224] Clemens, "First Fruits of a Barron Field", 23–4.

And warrants the creation
Of this fifth part of the Earth,
Which would seem an after-birth,
Not conceiv'd in the Beginning
(For GOD bless'd His work at first,
And saw that it was good),
But emerg'd at the first sinning,
When the ground was therefore curst;—
And hence this barren wood![225]

A blazon, French for "coat of arms", is a poem that catalogues the physical attributes of a subject, usually female, but Field's conquering male gaze is on "Australia", and specifically the kangaroo (a native animal on to which he narcissistically projects himself as colonial poetic creator of "this fifth part of the Earth"), and his pseudo-blazon is one in which the implied, already dismembered body parts (a coat of arms) of the monstrous kangaroo can only be (from the shocked coloniser's perspective) "Join'd by some divine mistake" (as with the techniques of his poems).[226] And so through the metaphorical cataloguing of other animals—first, through European mythical literary monstrosities (a "Sphynx or mermaid realiz'd", "a centaur unfabulous", a "Pegasus", a "hippogriff"—"chimeras all!"), and then through a combination of other living creatures (squirrel, deer and the camélopard (giraffe) "of the panther size"),[227] in addition to his suturing of the language of his European literary forebears, Field initiated a favourite national pastime of projecting The Master's language, specifically in poetic form, on to the Australian land to fetishise and reinforce the invader's claim to ownership.[228] He even hijacks Virgil's description of the Minotaur as his epigraph for "The Kangaroo": *Mixtumque genus, prolesque biformis* ("mixed birth and biform offspring") (*Aeneid*, 6.25). The kangaroo has since come to symbolise the "Spirit of

[225] Field, *First Fruits*, 7.

[226] Field, *First Fruits*, 8.

[227] Field, *First Fruits*, 7–8.

[228] For another instance among many, see "My Country" ("I love a sunburnt country / A land of sweeping plains") by British settler poet Dorothea Mackellar, which continues to be reappropriated in jingoistic advertisements. See also, for recent attempts to unsettle this poetic lineage, Toby Fitch (ed.), *Transforming My Country: A selection of poems responding to Dorothea Mackellar's "My Country"* (Australian Poetry Chapbook, 2017 and 2021), https://emergingwritersfestival.org.au/wp-content/uploads/2021/06/Transforming-My-Country_AP2021.pdf.

Australia", emblazoned as it is, white on red, on the aeroplane of Qantas, the national airline.

aussi

From the outset of "Australian poetry", via Field, there is an unconscious desire for monstrous artistic objects to represent and adapt to an antipodean, upside-down imaginary, yet the object(ive) of his poetry was employed for an inverted nefarious means—to establish the borders of this Down Under colony. In his distinct ambition to shape the future culture and society, Field's doggerel was advancing the monstrous project of colonialism by looking outward (back to British and European models), only looking inward to the difference and diversity of the continent to fetishise it.

or

The population of the nation still mostly lives on or near coastlines, notionally facing out. In the early twenty-first century Australia's shores are still symbolic barriers.[229] Despite being, since 1788, a land for migrants, the entire country has recently been excised from the migration zone so that asylum seekers can be "processed offshore".[230] Completely surrounded by water, Australia is literally an is-land, an isolate, as Foss writes: "Even with that island called 'continent'; the terror of isolation

[229] Successive governments have adopted an anti-refugee catch-cry, "Turn back the boats!" The lives of many refugees, or "boat people", risking the seas to seek asylum in Australia have been notionally "saved" (and those people on boats "intercepted" have been rerouted—to Gulag-like offshore processing centres or back to their countries of origin, where they often risk persecution). The loud and manipulative political rhetoric has only increased the sense that Australia is zealously protective of its borders, callously indifferent to those claiming asylum. Former immigration minister, and now former prime minister, Scott Morrison, for example, instructed Border Protection staff in 2013 to replace the phrase "asylum seeker" with "illegal maritime arrival" and "client" with "detainee". See Tom Clark, "Calling a boat person a spade: Australia's asylum seeker rhetoric", *The Conversation*, October 22, 2013, http://theconversation.com/calling-a-boat-person-a-spade-australias-asylum-seeker-rhetoric-19367.

[230] Melissa Phillips, "Out of sight, out of mind: Excising Australia from the migration zone", *The Conversation*, May 17, 2013, http://theconversation.com/out-of-sight-out-of-mind-excising-australia-from-the-migration-zone-14387.

merely grows in proportion to the size of its inner space. Big or little, islands die from the inwards out".[231]

aussi

Australia's body politic often privileges an unimpeachable sense of nationalism through a celebration of a distorted idea/ideal of the true or real Australia.[232] To advance any criticism of Australia is to become, somehow, and in some circles, "unAustralian". In a country where racism is rooted in the police force,[233] where Indigenous Australians are incarcerated at far more than ten times the proportion of non-Indigenous Australians (with many still being killed in custody without justice),[234] where asylum seekers are tortured in offshore prison camps, where Aboriginal sporting heroes are simultaneously cheered and jeered,[235] where sharks lurk in more headlines than in shipwrecks, where mining the reefs and the land for natural resources is more important than preserving them for environmental or cultural reasons, where explorers Burke and Wills died, discovering little more than what colonials would expect to find, and where the mirage of coastal living gives way to the driest continent in the world—it's important to reflect on the political implications of poetry such as that discussed in this essay: poetry generated

[231] Foss, "Theatrum Nondum Cognitorum", 35.

[232] Before he was ousted as prime minister of Australia, Tony Abbott of the Liberal Party opined "that everyone has got to be on Team Australia". It was broadly debated in the media what he meant exactly, whether it was anti-terrorist rhetoric, scaremongering, or something even more insidious to be applied to "everyday Australians". See Anne Summers, "Tony Abbott's Team Australia entrenches inequality", *Sydney Morning Herald*, August 23, 2014, http://www.smh.com.au/comment/tony-abbotts-team-australia-entrenches-inequality-20140821-106sdk.html.

[233] In August 2015, the Australian Border Force police unit set up the ominously named "Operation Fortitude", an operation that would have seen police stop people on the streets of Melbourne for random visa checks (a process that would have relied on racial profiling) had there not been a huge public protest. Political rhetoric, however, continues to push this racist agenda.

[234] Corrective Services, Australia, "National and state information about adult prisoners and community-based corrections, including legal status, custody type, Indigenous status and sex", September quarter, 2024.

[235] In 2015, AFL star Adam Goodes of the Sydney Swans was widely booed by opposing fans for miming an Aboriginal war dance on the field, while NRL star Jonathon Thurston was universally lauded for winning the premiership for his team the North Queensland Cowboys.

by paranomasia—by the difference and sameness in words; a poetry of multiplicity that questions truth, authority, and symbolic structures by understumbling through them, under*mining* them; poetry that "offers you up" a serious parody, *serio ludere*, a paradox in terms; a poetry of *un*reason that ultimately transgresses the boundaries of the Master, with the desire to dismantle subjectivity and identity-formation—the inverse of Barron Field's.

In "Living On: Borderlines", Derrida writes of the inability of "the institution"—in his case, the university—to accept the undecidable in language and in translation. But he's also talking about the nation state: "What this institution cannot bear is for anyone to tamper with language, meaning both the national language and, paradoxically, an ideal translatability that neutralizes this national language. *Nationalism* and *universalism*. What this institution cannot bear is a *transformation* that leaves intact neither of these two complementary poles" (my emphasis).[236]

or

What Australia sometimes cannot bear—what there seems little room for—is difference, ambiguity, the other. In the antipodes of the global south, Australia, once mistaken for an Abyss, carries on the colonial-capitalist project of the West—of its imperial master Great Britain, and of its cultural and political master the United States.

Both Mallarmé and Derrida defy the Master. In Mallarmé's case, he ditched his "Book of Books", of which only fragments survive, and, late in his writings, fragmented his verse—in Derrida's words, he opened up the "space of writing". The result was *Un Coup de dés*, a poem that attempts the impossible: to find a form that renders thought and chance into language. It demonstrated a kind of mastery that Mallarmé's poem simultaneously wishes to shake off, as in the metaphor that reverberates through the poem: the Master shaking his fist at the impossibility of abolishing chance. Derrida goes one step further in his continual wandering away from writing, from "the father" who cannot be questioned. Via the puncept and citational methodologies, his deconstructive writings wander away from writing (as

[236] Derrida, "Roundtable on Translation", 93–4.

authorial representor of truth). Debunking categories and genres, his work wavers and blurs the lines between literature and philosophy.

Altering the project, inverting the master—“UNCONSTITUTIONAL”—the methods of *or*-play, piracy and forgery employed by Brennan, Edwards and Tranter present a riposte to the Western (including the settler Australian) canon, to authorial representations of language. Their experiments in mistranslation also open up terrain that (settler) Australian poetry might traverse. In other words, by testing the materials of language(s), poetry can draw attention to the shaky nature—the unstable meanings and interchangeable structures—of language, the illicit affairs of writing as representation, the chaos of multiple tongues, rather than settling on the singular, or the ideal.

or

In opening up productive poetic terrains by “testing the materials”, perhaps we need to return to the multivalent definitions of the “experimental”. As Clemens writes:

> Its etymology is extremely suggestive: literally, a coming out of danger (*periculum*). Experiment is of course also closely related to the modern English words experience and expert. They all derive from the Latin verb *experiri*, “to try”. That verb is itself a composite, from *ex*-, out of, and *periri*, the present passive infinitive of *pereo*; *pereo* means to pass away, to vanish, to perish. Ex-periment (and experience) is therefore a coming-out-of or a passing-through-danger. On this basis, we could then define an experiment as something like: the emergent inscription and transmission of an artificially-produced hazardous event at the limits of the known … Perhaps even more bizarrely, through the bizarre destinies of linguistic transmission, it turns out that the words experiment and pirate share the same root: “classical Latin *pirate* < Hellenistic Greek *peirates* < ancient Greek *peiran* to attempt, to attack, assault (<*peira* trial, attempt, endeavour: see *peirameter*, n.) + *-tes*, suffix forming agent nouns).” OED … An experimenter is therefore literally also an ex-pirate—which may also

> make us think of *expirate* (a 17th century word for breathing-out) and expire (a contemporary word for dying).[237]

or

As Carruthers puts it, "the word 'experiment', with its hints at piracy, death and danger, retain appropriate semes for the settler-colonial context".[238] Language is unstable—borders between languages, even within a language, are permeable. Homophony breathes the littoral/literal and tra*verses* the dangerous borders between languages. Through interpenetration, the experiment inherent in mistranslation cedes the initiative to words, which allows for changeability and transformation. Its implications are for a poetry that is open in form but not formless, diverse in character, and continually malleable. When thought of as transformational experimentation, mistranslation is both reverential and disrespectful (the mistranslator as an ex-pirate). It is an upending and re-reading that initiates alternative ways to traverse the multiplicities of language, history and tradition (the canon), and of time and place (real and imaginary).

aussi

Australian poet Peter Minter recommends a radical revision of approaches to reading local poetic traditions. Instead of a single authorial nation or nationality through which to view Australian poetry, Minter proposes an "archipelagic map": "Rather than 'the Land' and its monocultural aesthetic, we might imagine a polyphony of terrestrial islands, archipelagos of *habitus* and poethical emergence".[239] Quoting Édouard Glissant's *Poetics of Relation*, each island in Minter's vision becomes

> an outcrop of sensibility amidst oceans of inscrutability, or what … Édouard Glissant termed the *chaos-monde*. A crucial stage in the emergence of a poetics of relation, the *chaos-monde* (chaos world) is the liberation of the world from representability: "the way Chaos

[237] Clemens, in email correspondence with A.J. Carruthers, "1897 in 1981: Stéphane Mallarmé avec Christopher Brennan", 90.

[238] Carruthers, "1897 in 1981: Stéphane Mallarmé avec Christopher Brennan", 90.

[239] Peter Minter, "Archipelagos of sense: thinking about a decolonised Australian poetics", *Southerly* 73.1 (2013): 160.

> itself goes around is the opposite of what is ordinarily understood by 'chaotic' and … it opens a new phenomenon: Relation, or totality in evolution, whose order is continually in flux and this disorder one can imagine forever". The whole world is an archipelago, representability cohering at the edges of ever shifting shores.[240]

In terms of the aesthetic potential of an archipelagic model, Minter leaves this open-ended, preferring to outline the theoretical, cultural and psychogeographical implications, but I think it is clear how *Un Coup de dés* and its typographical and semantic *chaos-monde*, its scattered fragments in flux and relation, has created an archipelagic map that appeals to settler Australian poets seeking otherness and indeterminacy, and a poetic map that allows for rebellion, shadowplay, and the chaos and echoes of the multilingual.

or

The poem as *echo*pelago.

aussi

Foss describes maps as "stratagems for the abolition of distance … They constitute vanishing lines, escape machines, a beacon of fascination", phrases that could also describe "A Fluke", "Musicopoematographoscope", or "Desmond's Coupé". Foss goes on: "maps may be an empty simulation, as in the most beautiful imaginings of Plato … which, even if … not meant as reality, certainly had the effect of sending countless men in search of new lands over the ages and contributed to the way in which they were shaped". Maps as empty simulations is not useful here (more on this below), however a third and final description of maps by Foss is relevant, in terms of a metaphor for the poem as a space for interchange and fluidity: "what they refer to or give bearing to is not territory as a fixed substance, but territory as fluid field".[241] And so we come full circle, tail in mouth (tongue in cheek), to Brownian Motion.

[240] Minter, "Archipelagos of sense", 156. For more on Glissant's *chaos-monde*, see Édouard Glissant, *Poetics of Relation*, trans. Betsy Wing (Ann Arbor: University of Michigan Press, 1997).

[241] Foss, "Theatrum Nondum Cognitorum", 22–3.

or

In the fluid field of the page, archipelagos emerge, scattered fragments swerve, invisible filaments waver, various and other histories echo, words intertextualise, disappear and reappear slightly altered, othered (yet *in relation* to one another for their very being there, their materiality).

or

How much can the poem-map be explored? Thinking of the poem as an exploration sounds innocent enough, but exploration has its problems or limitations, particularly in the Australian postcolonial context (in which colonial exploration by white Europeans is not only recent history, but celebrated history), and therefore by extension in the context of rewritings and appropriation by/of Australian writers. These connotations (of the word exploration—that of men in power infiltrating a supposed *terra nullius* that is not *terra nullius* so as to turn Indigenous country into an empty simulation, a colony) serve as warning to those seeking power, control, dominion and domination, in the intertextual exploration and appropriation of another's writing. Defy Mallarmé's Master, sure, but beware of becoming the master.

aussi

To turn to the "erotics" of language in this regard, particularly to that of the highly libidinal nature of language-tampering, but also of the oscillation-dissolution of the "I" into the "other" into "them", one can thereby also too rapidly dissolve certain political them(e)atics at stake in appropriation: perhaps most notably in the context of sexuality and race.

All the rewritings I've examined in this essay are men-rewriting-men, albeit through differing subjectivities, which at the very least exhibits a homo*social* lineage, of an a-sexualised-material-able-to-be-resampled-without-any-prohibition-but-custom-and-copyright. Of this a-sexualised material in *Un Coup de dés*, Tranter concocts a kind of alpha-male-alpha-poet stoush (with the Romantic Adamson-cum-Mallarmé), while Edwards subverts it with an illicit affair (with language) in which a homosexual subjectivity is at stake, if that hasn't yet been obvious in my analysis, and which clearly has a more political resonance. But this then may suggest that even such samplings also operate some covert elisions: for instance, is "women's poetry" able to be re-cited by men today with the same effect? Or vice-versa? Absolutely to the latter, as there are feminist and queer contexts to the rewriting of phallocentrism, an upending or dispersion of a patriarchal hegemony. But hetero men rewriting/overwriting/appropriating women's poetry…? That's another fettle of kitsch, so to speak, an unwanted/unwarranted inversion of feminism, and would come with a different set of variables and boundaries. As I've tried to establish, there are many excellent queer displacements that exist, in regards to appropriation in literature; however, I don't mean to gloss over the fact that all writers, regardless of sexual orientation or desire, have ethical responsibilities.

aussi

Ditto for racial and colonial issues, as I've implied in this coda. I'm thinking now of the American poet Kenneth Goldsmith's 2015 reading at Brown University in which Goldsmith spent thirty minutes reading the autopsy report of Michael Brown, a young African-American man killed by police.[242] This "poetry" reading was absolutely a kind of literary appropriation, and one that was presented as if verbatim, as if the autopsy report was being entirely re-contextualised (a technique Goldsmith employs across his oeuvre) to highlight (through the mundanity of the language structures appropriated) the mundanity in this case of the mounting deaths of black African-Americans at the hands of mostly white police. The intention was perhaps valid, but when Goldsmith ended the reading with a description of Brown's genitalia, it became clear that he had deliberately edited the autopsy for shock value, thus representing (and so repeating) a blatant accentuation of white domination (and fetishisation) of black bodies. One could argue (and Goldsmith has, convincingly to some) that this was the point (he did in fact introduce his reading as being of a poem called "The Body of Michael Brown", and then justified it as a formal conceit—he was

[242] Jillian Steinhauer, "Kenneth Goldsmith Remixes Michael Brown Autopsy Report as Poetry", *Hyperallergic*, March 16, 2015, http://hyperallergic.com/190954/kenneth-goldsmith-remixes-michael-brown-autopsy-report-as-poetry/.

writing a blazon![243]), but he was subsequently and rightly criticised—by African-Americans and non-anglo and anglo Americans alike—for his performance's illicit appropriations (of the injustices) of black experience in contemporary America for further white self-aggrandisement.[244]

or

The problem of the limits of appropriability is clearly then a major and intense and ongoing international discussion, and one that will continue. In most situations, the limits are not so much a question of taste as power. The abject in Edwards works because it is redirected through his own queer subjectivity in the face of traditional, cis literary power structures, whereas the abject in Goldsmith merely apes his white privilege, even as he employs an extreme style of appropriation to challenge traditional literary forms.

So while I've been advocating for certain boundaries/borders of the imagination, traditional and aesthetic and emotional, to be breached, demolished or abolished, there are always some specific social, cultural and historical boundaries/borders that need to be treated with ethical respect. Going beyond can be painful to certain others (to re-echo Bataille's erotic philosophy, as he refers to anguish): "when the bounds of the possible are over-reached, a recoil is inevitable".[245] In other words, sometimes the defiance of the master may under certain circumstances require stringent self-limitation in the appropriation of others' texts. There are symbolic barriers that need dissolving, and others that need shoring up.

or

As Savige writes, "Australian poetry harbors more monsters than Pliny the Elder could poke a stick at, and it undoubtedly finds itself at home with a radical recombinant poetics that is by turns (mis)translational,

[243] Alison Flood, "US poet defends reading of Michael Brown autopsy report as a poem", *The Guardian*, March 18, 2015, https://www.theguardian.com/books/2015/mar/17/michael-brown-autopsy-report-poem-kenneth-goldsmith.

[244] See CAConrad, "Kenneth Goldsmith Says He Is an Outlaw", *Poetry Foundation*, June 1, 2015, https://www.poetryfoundation.org/harriet/2015/06/kenneth-goldsmith-says-he-is-an-outlaw/. Here, thirty poets of multiple racial and sexual orientations strongly object to Goldsmith's appropriation of the deceased and black body of Michael Brown.

[245] Bataille, *Eroticism*, 87.

heteronymous, and even cannibalistic, in the way of Hannibal Lecte[u] r"[246] (an allusion to Edwards' Preface to "A Fluke" in which the speaker professes, at least self-consciously: "I wish I knew what lunatic pasted this Note here—*park it elsewhere, I say*—these maimed, oblivious and hellish apprehensions remind me of Hannibal Lecter."[247]). Savige goes on, alluding to Barron Field: "The cannibal poet may be a self-negating monster—'on Creation's holiday,' this is celebrated [...] The self-negating figure of the poet of any stripe is a strange kind of *mixtumque genus*: the poet 'monsters' silence, and is monstered by it in return." Indeed, and this is the context Australian poetry will never, never be able to escape. Australia is a land built on theft. How to write about, around and through this theft, that is the Circular Quay.

or

And here I return to the pun as subversive device, whose tidiness plays with the illusion of mastery at the same time as undoing it. At its core, the puncept is a methodology that, to bring back Ulmer, "allows language to say what it knows, which allows the unconscious to show itself in the play of language", [248] and thus and most often reveal authorial intent.

aussi

Plato's Republic never physically existed, yet the utopian Atlantis myth he instigated (as a literal Antipodes, an "opposite earth") and the Republic as a concept (Australia is not yet a Republic, a future event that might inversely open itself up to new inclusivities, but its exclusion of Indigenous poetry for most of its colonial history echoes Plato's Republic's exclusion of poets)[249] still persists on Australian shores, and the colony still generally

[246] Savige, "'Creation's Holiday'".

[247] Edwards, "Preface", in *A Fluke*, n.p.

[248] Ulmer, "The Puncept in Grammatology", 175.

[249] See Carruthers, who writes, "If Antipodal literature is based firmly upon tradition in an Aboriginal sense, before a modern and colonial one, for non-Aboriginal Australians the spectre of a barred Republic casts a shadow over the Australian verse tradition." In Carruthers, "1897 in 1981: Stéphane Mallarmé avec Christopher Brennan", 87. I am also fully aware that the protagonists of this essay don't directly address Indigenous Australian politics in their Mallarmé anti-versions—their work rather addresses "the spectre of a barred Republic" in generative ways, aesthetically and conceptually, for what it's worth.

thinks of its centre as void. Its being void is a furphy and delusion, of course—abundant life, Aboriginal communities, and Dreamtime tracks resonate like filaments through its many Indigenous nations, whether in the "Outback" or not.

To overturn any anxious anglo-colonial readings and Eurovisions—any unease that readers, writers and critics might have about the legitimacy of antipodean takes on cultural internationalism—and, furthermore, to alleviate the stress of repressing unpleasant colonial truths, settler Australian poetry could do more than simply breathe the *littoral* (or the literal), however utopian that might seem; Australian poetry should breathe the littoral *and* the void, the never never (the impossible), by ceding the initiative to words *and* space. Engaging the materiality of words and the space of the page (while *re*membering social, cultural and historical underpinnings with respect) can assist in unearthing the untenability of the logocentric and phallocentric distinction between the sensible and the intelligible, between the ideal and the material, the singular and the multiple. Using an inverse logic, misprision removes the prison, danger undoes the dungeon. As Mallarmé ceded at the end, art must embrace the risk that comes with chance, as chance will never be abolished.

or

For settler Australian poetry to create notions (archipelagos, say, as opposed to a single nation) of itself, from out of (or within) the *terra nullius* myth that has been perpetuated—it must invert and disperse the hemispheres. It must simultaneously reflect (not reject!) the abject—in order to transform, in order to live—and look within (into the never).

Fin

Bibliography

Adamson, Robert. "The Truth I Know: An Interview with Robert Adamson by John Tranter". *Makar* 14.1 (1978): 3–13.

Adorno, Theodor W. "Subject-Object". In *Aesthetic Theory*, 1970, translated by Robert Hullot-Kentor, 223–39. Minneapolis: University of Minnesota Press, 1998.

Anderson, Jill, ed. *Australian Divagations: Mallarmé & the 20th Century*. New York: Peter Lang Publishing, 2002.

Armand, Louis. "Constellations". In *Literate Technologies: Language, Cognition & Technics*, 97–131. Prague: Litteraria Pragensia, 2006.

Armand, Louis, ed. "Introduction: Transversions of the Contemporary" in *Contemporary Poetics*, ii–xiii. Evanston: Northwestern University Press, 2007.

Armand, Louis. *Technē: James Joyce, Hypertext & Technology*. Univerzita Karlova v Praze, Nakladatelství Karolinum, 2003.

Armand, Louis, ed. *VLAK* 5, 2015.

Attwood, Bain. "Unsettling pasts: reconciliation and history in settler Australia". *Postcolonial Studies* 8.3 (2015): 243–59. http://dx.doi.org/10.1080/13688790500231012.

Badiou, Alain. *Being and Event*. 1998. Translated by Oliver Feltham. New York: Continuum, 2005.

Barnes, Katherine. "'With a smile barely wrinkling the surface': Christopher Brennan's Large Musicopoematographoscope and Mallarmé's *Un Coup de dés*". *XIX: Dix-Neuf*, Number 9 (October 2007): 44–56. http://www.ingentaconnect.com.ezp.lib.unimelb.edu.au/content/maney/dix/2007/00000009/00000001/art00004.

Barthes, Roland. *Image-Music-Text*. Translated by Stephen Heath. London: Fontana, 1977.

Bataille, Georges. *Eroticism*. 1962. Translated by Mary Dalwood. London: Marion Boyars, 1987.

Bataille, Georges. "The Solar Anus". In *Visions of Excess: Selected Writings, 1927-1939*, edited and translated by Allan Stoekl, 5–9. Minneapolis: University of Minnesota Press, 1985.

Bataille, Georges. *Story of the Eye*. 1963. Translated by Joachim Neugroschal. Harmondsworth: Penguin, 1979.

Bate, W. Jackson. *The Burden of the Past and the English Poet*. London: Chatto & Windus, 1971.

Beckett, Samuel. *Comment C'est How It Is And / et L'image: A Critical-Genetic Edition*. Edited by Edouard Magessa O'Reilly. New York and London: Routledge, 2001.

Benjamin, Walter. *Illuminations*. 1955. Translated by Harry Zohn. 1968. London: Fontana, 1992.

Bernstein, Charles. *The Practice of Poetry: Writing Exercises from Poets Who Teach*. Edited by Robin Behn and Twichell Chase. New York: Harper, 1992.

Bjelić, Dušan I. "Balkan Geography and the De-Orientalization of Freud". *Journal of Modern Greek Studies* 29.1 (May 2011): 27–49.

Bloom, Harold. *The Anxiety of Influence: A Theory of Poetry*, Second Edition. New York: Oxford University Press, 1997.

Bloom, Harold. *A Map of Misreading*. New York: Oxford University Press, 1975.

Bonahon, Francis. *Low-Dimensional Geometry: from Euclidean Surfaces to Hyperbolic Knots*. Providence: American Mathematical Society, 2009.

Boncardo, Robert. *Mallarme and the Politics of Literature: Sartre, Kristeva, Badiou, Ranciere*. Edinburgh: Edinburgh University Press, 2019.

Boncardo, Robert and Christian R. Gelder. *Mallarmé: Rancière, Milner, Badiou*. Lanham: Rowman & Littlefield, 2018.

Brachet, Auguste. *An Etymological Dictionary of the French Language*. Translated by G. W. Kitchin. Oxford: Clarendon, 1873.

Brennan, Christopher. *Poems 1913*. Sydney: Angus & Robertson, 1992.

Brennan, Christopher. *Prose-Verse-Poster-Algebraic-Symbolico-Riddle Musicopoematographoscope & Pocket Musicopoematographoscope*. Erskineville: Hale & Iremonger, 1981.

Broodthaers, Marcel. *Un Coup de dés jamais n'abolira le hasard*. Artist's book, offset lithograph on transparent paper. Cologne, Antwerp: Wide White Space Gallery; Galerie Michael Werner, 1969.

Brooks, David. “Feral Symbolists: Robert Adamson, John Tranter, and the Response to Rimbaud”. *Australian Literary Studies* 16.3 (1994).

Brooks, David. “Field’s Kangaroo”. *Kenyon Review* (March/April 2017).

Brooks, David. *The Sons of Clovis: Ern Malley, Adoré Floupette and a Secret History of Australian Poetry*. St. Lucia: University of Queensland Press, 2011.

Burgess, Gelett. *The Burgess Nonsense Book*. New York: Frederick A. Stokes Company, 1901.

Butler, Judith. *Gender Trouble: Feminism and the Subversion of Identity*. New York: Routledge, 1990.

CAConrad. “Kenneth Goldsmith Says He Is an Outlaw”. *Poetry Foundation*. June 1, 2015. https://www.poetryfoundation.org/harriet/2015/06/kenneth-goldsmith-says-he-is-an-outlaw/.

Carson, Anne. *Nay Rather*, The Cahiers Series #21. London: Sylph Editions, 2013.

Carruthers, A. J. *Literary History and Avant-Garde Poetics in the Antipodes: Languages of Invention*. Edinburgh: Edinburgh Critical Studies in Avant-Garde Writing, Edinburgh University Press, 2024.

Catullus, Gaius Valerius. *The Poems of Catullus: A Bilingual Edition*. Translated by Peter Green. Berkeley: University of California Press, 2007.

Clark, Tom. “Calling a boat person a spade: Australia’s asylum seeker rhetoric”. *The Conversation*, October 22, 2013. http://theconversation.com/calling-a-boat-person-a-spade-australias-asylum-seeker-rhetoric-19367.

Clarke, Donovan. “Michael Massey Robinson”. In *Australian Dictionary of Biography*, Vol. 2, 1967, and online 2006. https://adb.anu.edu.au/biography/robinson-michael-massey-2598.

Clemens, Justin. “First Fruits of a Barron Field”. *Critical Quarterly* (May 14, 2019). https://doi.org/10.1111/criq.12451.

Clemens, Justin, and Thomas H. Ford. *Barron Field in New South Wales: The Poetics of Terra Nullius*. Melbourne: Melbourne University Press, 2023.

Clinefelter, Jim. *A Throw of the Snore Will Surge the Potatoes: John M. Bennett meets Stéphane Mallarmé*. Columbus, Ohio: Luna Bisonte Productions, 1998.

Cloud, Random. "Fearful Assymetry". In *The Cambridge Companion to Textual Scholarship*, edited by Neil Fraistat and Julia Flanders, 134–87. Cambridge: Cambridge University Press, 2013.

Corrective Services, Australia. "National and state information about adult prisoners and community-based corrections, including legal status, custody type, Indigenous status and sex". September quarter, 2024.

Culler, Jonathan. *The Pursuit of Signs: Semiotics, Literature, Deconstruction*. London: Routledge & Kegan Paul, 1981.

Derrida, Jacques. *Dissemination*. Translated, with an Introduction and Additional Notes, by Barbara Johnson. London: Althone Press, 1981.

Derrida, Jacques. "The Double Session". 1972. In *Dissemination*, translated by Barbara Johnson, 173–286. Chicago: University of Chicago Press, 1981.

Derrida, Jacques. "The Law of Genre". Translated by Avital Ronell. *Glyph: Textual Studies* 7 (1980): 202–32.

Derrida, Jacques. "Mallarmé". 1974. Translated by Christine Roulston. In *Acts of Literature*, edited by Derek Attridge, 110–26. London: Routledge, 1991.

Derrida, Jacques. *Of Grammatology*. 1967. Translated by Gayatri Chakravorty Spivak. Baltimore: Johns Hopkins University Press, 1997.

Derrida, Jacques. *Positions*. 1972. Translated by Alan Bass. Chicago: University of Chicago Press: 1981.

Derrida, Jacques. "Roundtable on Translation". 1982. In *The Ear of the Other*, translated by Christie McDonald, 91–161. Lincoln: University of Nebraska Press, 1988.

Doherty, Brian, ed. *Aspen Magazine in a Box (for Stéphane Mallarmé][a.k.a. The Minimalism Issue]*. 5 + 6, Fall/Winter (1967).

DuPlessis, Rachel Blau. *POESIS*. Houston, Texas: Little Red Leaves Textile Series, 2016.

Edwards, Chris. *After Naptime: A Poem, Profusely Illustrated*. Marrickville: Vagabond Press, Stray Dog Editions, 2014.

Edwards, Chris. "Double Talk". Paper presented at the Sydney Poetry Seminar on "Poetry and Authenticity", May 20-21, 2005. *Poetry International Web* (Nov 1, 2006). http://www.poetryinternationalweb.net/pi/site/cou_article/item/7929/Double-Talk/en.

Edwards, Chris. *A Fluke: A mistranslation of Stéphane Mallarmé's "Un coup de dés…" with parallel French pretext.* Thirroul: Monogene, 2005.

Edwards, Chris. "Interview with Chris Edwards". Edited by Michael Brennan. *Poetry International Web* (July 1, 2011). http://www.poetryinternationalweb.net/pi/site/cou_article/item/19012/Interview-with-Chris-Edwards/en.

Edwards, Chris. *People of Earth: poems.* Marrickville: Vagabond Press, 2011.

Edwards, Chris, and Toby Fitch. "*After Naptime* Launch Interview". Vagabond Xmas Party, Gleebooks, Sydney, December 7, 2014.

Einstein, Albert. *Investigations on the Theory of the Brownian Movement.* Translated by A. D. Cowper. 1926. Mineola: Dover, 1956. http://users.physik.fu-berlin.de/~kleinert/files/eins_brownian.pdf.

Fagan, Kate. "'A Fluke? [N]ever!': Reading Chris Edwards". *JASAL* 12.1 (2012). http://www.nla.gov.au/ojs/index.php/jasal/article/view/2270.

Fagan, Kate, and Peter Minter. "Murdering Alphabets, Disorienting Romance: John Tranter and Postmodern Australian Poetics". *Jacket* 27 (April 2005). http://jacketmagazine.com/27/faga-mint.html.

Farrell, Michael. "Rebellious Tropes: Michael Farrell on Toby Fitch". *Sydney Review of Books* (May 2020). https://sydneyreviewofbooks.com/reviews/rebellious-tropes.

Farrell, Michael. *Writing Australian Unsettlement: Modes of Poetic Invention 1796-1945.* New York: Palgrave MacMillan, 2015.

Field, Barron. *First Fruits of Australian Poetry.* Sydney: Printed by George Howe, 1819. Barron Field. *First Fruits*, 2nd edition. Sydney: Printed by R. Howe, 1823.

Fitch, Toby. "Plagiarism scandal has revealed an ugly side of Australian poetry". *The Guardian*, September 23, 2013. http://www.theguardian.com/commentisfree/2013/sep/23/australian-poetry-plagiarism.

Fitch, Toby. *The Bloomin' Notions of Other & Beau.* Marrickville: Vagabond Press, 2014.

Fitch, Toby, ed. *Transforming My Country: A selection of poems responding to Dorothea Mackellar's "My Country"* (Australian Poetry Chapbook, 2017 and 2021), https://emergingwritersfestival.org.au/wp-content/uploads/2021/06/Transforming-My-Country_AP2021.pdf.

Flood, Alison. "US poet defends reading of Michael Brown autopsy report as a poem". *The Guardian*. March 18, 2015. https://www.theguardian.com/books/2015/mar/17/michael-brown-autopsy-report-poem-kenneth-goldsmith.

Foss, Paul. "Theatrum Nondum Cognitorum". In *Foreign Bodies Papers*, edited by Peter Botsman, Chris Burns and Peter Hutchings, 15–38. Sydney: Local Consumption Publications, 1981.

Freud, Sigmund. *Jokes and Their Relation to the Unconscious*. Vol. 6 of the Pelican Freud Library. 1905. Translated by James Strachey. New York: W. W. Norton, 1960.

Freud, Sigmund. *The Psychopathology of Everyday Life*. Vol. 5 of the Pelican Freud Library. Translated by Alan Tyson. 1960. Harmondsworth: Penguin, 1975.

Fuller, Loïe and Brygida Ochaim. *La Danse des couleurs*. Bienale de la danse, 1988. https://numeridanse.com/en/publication/loie-fuller-la-danse-des-couleurs-3/.

Genette, Gérard. *Palimpsests: Literature in the Second Degree*. 1982. Translated by Channa Newman and Claude Doubinsky. Lincoln: University of Nebraska Press, 1997.

Glissant, Édouard. *Poetics of Relation*. 1990. Translated by Betsy Wing. Ann Arbor: University of Michigan Press, 1997.

Goldsmith, Kenneth. *Uncreative Writing*. New York: Columbia University Press, 2011.

Greene, Roland et al., eds. *The Princeton Encyclopedia of Poetry and Poetics: Fourth Edition*. Princeton: Princeton University Press, 2012.

Guest, Stephanie. "Nothing's Lost: Towards a Poetics of Transnational Unoriginality in Australian Poetry". Honours thesis, Department of English, University of Sydney, 2013.

Guriel, Jason. "A Poet Turned Michael Brown's Autopsy Report Into Click-Bait as Performance Art". *New Republic*. March 25, 2015. https://newrepublic.com/article/121364/how-should-we-think-about-kenneth-goldsmiths-poetic-remixes.

Hawke, John. *Australian Literature and the Symbolist Movement*. Wollongong: University of Wollongong Press, 2009.

Horáček, Josef. "Pedantry and Play: The Zukofsky *Catullus*". *Comparative Literature Studies* 51.1 (2014): 106–31.

Jones, Susan. "A Poetics of Potentiality: Mallarmé, Fuller, Yeats, and Graham". In *Literature, Modernism, and Dance*, 13–43. Oxford: Oxford University Press, 2013.

Joyce, James. *Finnegans Wake*. Harmondsworth: Penguin, 1999.

Joyce, James. *Ulysses: The 1922 Text*. New York: University of Oxford Press, 2008.

Kant, Immanuel. *Critique of Pure Reason*. 1781. Translated by J. M. D. Meiklejohn. New York: Dover, 2003.

Kristeva, Julia. *The Kristeva Reader*. Edited by Toril Moi. New York: Columbia University Press, 1986.

Kristeva, Julia. *Powers of Horror: An Essay on Abjection*. 1980. Translated by Leon S. Roudiez. New York: Columbia University Press, 1982.

Lacan, Jacques. *Anxiety: The Seminar of Jacques Lacan Book X*. Edited by Jacques Alain-Miller, translated by A. R. Price. Cambridge: Polity Press, 2014.

Lacan, Jacques. *The Four Fundamental Conceptions of Psychoanalysis*. 1973. Translated by Alan Sheridan. London: Hogarth, 1977.

Lacan, Jacques. *The Other Side of Psychoanalysis: The Seminar of Jacques Lacan, Book XVII*. Translated by Russell Grigg. New York: W. W. Norton & Company, 2010.

Lacan, Jacques. "Seminar on 'The Purloined Letter'". *Yale French Studies* 0.48 (1972). http://xroads.virginia.edu/~DRBR2/lacan2.pdf.

Lamb, Charles. "Review of Barron Field, *First Fruits of Australian Poetry* (1819)". *Examiner*, January 16, 1820.

Lindsay, Lionel. "Christopher Bennan lost his post at Sydney University through drink and an adventure". *News*, Adelaide, December 3, 1954. https://trove.nla.gov.au/newspaper/article/131218020.

McCooey, David. "Review Short: John Tranter's *Heart Starter*". *Cordite Poetry Review* (August 25, 2015). http://cordite.org.au/reviews/mccooey-tranter/.

"Mabo v Queensland", No. 2. HCA 23. 175 CLR 1 (June 3, 1992).

Mallarmé, Stéphane. *Collected Poems*. Translated and with a commentary by Henry Weinfield. Berkeley: University of California Press, 1996.

Mallarmé, Stéphane. *Un Coup de dés jamais n'abolira le hasard.* 1897. Paris: Gallimard, 1914.

Mallarmé, Stéphane. *Divagations.* 1897. Translated by Barbara Johnson. Cambridge: Belknap, 2007.

Mallarmé, Stéphane. *Selected Letters of Stéphane Mallarmé.* Edited and translated by Rosemary Lloyd. Chicago: Chicago University Press, 1988.

Manne, Robert, ed. *Whitewash: On Keith Windschuttle's Fabrication of Aboriginal History.* Collingwood: Black Inc., 2003.

Mathews, Harry. "Translation and the Oulipo: The Case of the Persevering Maltese". *Electronic Book Review.* March 1, 1997. https://electronicbookreview.com/essay/translation-and-the-oulipo-the-case-of-the-persevering-maltese/.

Milliken, Robert. "Keating's rear view of the lucky country causes storm: Careless remarks have damaged the PM's nationalist stance". *Independent,* June 27, 1994. http://www.independent.co.uk/news/world/keatings-rear-view-of-the-lucky-country-causes-storm-careless-remarks-have-damaged-the-pms-1425378.html.

Minter, Peter. "Archipelagos of sense: thinking about a decolonised Australian poetics". *Southerly* 73.1 (2013): 155–69.

Musgrave, David. "Paris, Capital of the Australian Poetic Avant-Garde: Christopher Brennan's 'Musicopoematographoscope's John Tranter's' 'Desmond's Coupé' and Chris Edwards' 'A Fluke' and *After Naptime*". In Alistair Rolls, ed. *Remembering Paris: Echoes of Baudelaire in Text and on Screen,* 165–86. Bristol and Chicago: Intellect, 2021.

Newton, Isaac. *Newton's Principia: the mathematical principles of natural philosophy.* Translated by Andrew Motte. New York: Daniel Adee, 1846.

Nietzsche, Friedrich. *The Gay Science.* 1887. Translated by Walter Kaufmann. New York: Vintage, 1974.

Olson, Charles. "Logography". In *Additional Prose: A Bibliography on America, Proprioception & Other Notes & Essays,* edited by George F. Butterick. Bolinas: Four Seasons Foundation, 1974.

Oxford English Dictionary. 2nd ed. 20 vols. Oxford: Oxford University Press, 1989.

Paz, Octavio. *Alternating Current.* 1967. Translated by Helen R. Lane. New York: Viking, 1973.

Pearson, Roger. *Mallarmé and Circumstance: The Translation of Silence*. Clarendon: Oxford University Press, 2004.

Perrin, Jean. *Atoms*. 1914. Translated by Dalziel Llewellyn Hammick. London: Constable, 1916.

Phillips, Melissa. "Out of sight, out of mind: Excising Australia from the migration zone". *The Conversation*, May 17, 2013. http://theconversation.com/out-of-sight-out-of-mind-excising-australia-from-the-migration-zone-14387.

Plato. *The Republic*. Translated by Desmond Lee. 1955. Harmondsworth: Penguin, 1987.

Pollack, John. *The Pun Also Rises: How the Humble Pun Revolutionized Language, Changed History, and Made Wordplay More than Some Antics*. New York: Gotham, 2012.

Porter, Peter. "Saving from the Wreck". In *Saving from the Wreck*, 23–48. Nottingham: Trent, 2001.

Pound, Ezra. *The Cantos of Ezra Pound*. 1934. New York: New Directions, 1993.

Rancière, Jacques. *Mallarmé: The Politics of the Siren*. 1996. Translated by Steve Corcoran. London: Continuum, 2011.

Rasula, Jed, and Steve McCaffery, eds. *Imagining Language: An Anthology*. Cambridge: MIT Press, 1998.

Redfern, Walter. *Puns: Second Edition*. Harmondsworth: Penguin, 2000.

Saussure, Ferdinand de. *Course in General Linguistics*. 1893. Translated by Wade Baskin. New York: Columbia University Press, 2011.

Savige, Jaya. "Creation's Holiday". *Poetry Magazine*. May 2, 2016. https://www.poetryfoundation.org/poetrymagazine/articles/89027/creations-holiday-on-silence-and-monsters-in-australian-poetry.

"Signorelli parapraxis". *Wikipedia*. https://en.wikipedia.org/wiki/Signorelli_parapraxis.

Starobinski, Jean. *Words Upon Words: The Anagrams of Ferdinand Saussure*. 1971. Translated by Olivia Emmet. New Haven: Yale University Press, 1979.

Steiner, George. *After Babel: Aspects of Language and Translation*. Oxford: Oxford University Press, 1975.

Steinhauer, Jillian. "Kenneth Goldsmith Remixes Michael Brown Autopsy Report as Poetry". *Hyperallergic*. March 16, 2015. http://hyperallergic.com/190954/kenneth-goldsmith-remixes-michael-brown-autopsy-report-as-poetry/.

Summers, Anne. "Tony Abbott's Team Australia entrenches inequality". *Sydney Morning Herald*, August 23, 2014. http://www.smh.com.au/comment/tony-abbotts-team-australia-entrenches-inequality-20140821-106sdk.html.

Tranter, John. "Brennan's Tinker's damn". Review of *Prose-Verse-Poster-Algebraic-Symbolico-Riddle Musicopoematographoscope & Pocket Musicopoematographoscope* by Christopher Brennan. *Jacket* 29 (April 2006). http://johntranter.com/reviewer/1982-brennan-oscope.shtml.

Tranter, John. "Distant Voices". Doctor of Creative Arts Thesis, School of Journalism and Creative Writing, University of Wollongong (2009). http://ro.uow.edu.au/theses/3191/.

Tranter, John. *Starlight: 150 poems*. St Lucia: University of Queensland Press, 2010.

Tymoczko, Maria. *Enlarging Translation, Empowering Translators*. Manchester: St. Jerome, 2007.

Ulmer, Gregory. "The Puncept in Grammatology". In *On Puns: The Foundation of Letters*. Edited by Jonathan Culler. Oxford: Basil Blackwell, 1988.

"Unicron", *Wikipedia*. https://en.wikipedia.org/wiki/Unicron.

Weinfield, Henry. "'Thinking out afresh the whole poetic problem': Brennan's Prescience; Mallarmé's Accomplishment". *Southerly* 68.3 (2008): 10–26.

Yeats, William Butler. *Mythologies*. London: Macmillan, 1924.

Zukofsky, Ceila Thaew, and Louis Zukovsky. *Catullus [Gai Valeri Catulli Veronensis Liber]*. London: Cape Golliard, 1969.

www.ingramcontent.com/pod-product-compliance
Lightning Source LLC
Chambersburg PA
CBHW032055090426
42744CB00005B/226
* 9 7 8 1 9 1 6 5 4 1 1 8 4 *